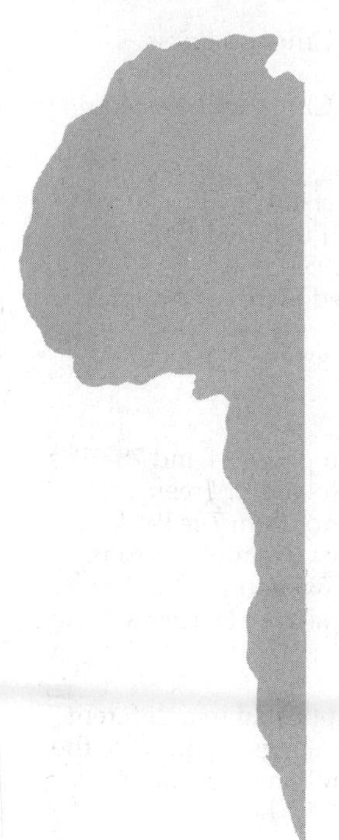

The Journey Back

Issues in Black Literature and Criticism

Houston A. Baker, Jr.

The University of Chicago Press
Chicago and London

THE UNIVERSITY OF CHICAGO PRESS, CHICAGO 60637
THE UNIVERSITY OF CHICAGO PRESS, LTD., LONDON

Paperback edition 1983
Printed in the United States of America

90 89 88 87 86 85 84 83   2 3 4 5 6

Parts of chapter 4 appeared in a different form in " 'These are songs if you have the music': An Essay on Imamu Baraka," *Minority Voices* 1 (1977): 1–18.

Library of Congress Cataloging in Publication Data

Baker, Houston A
The journey back.

Includes bibliographical references and index.
1. American literature—Afro-American authors—History and criticism. I. Title.
PS153.N5B24   810'.9'896073
79–20861
ISBN 0-226-03534-4 (cloth)
0-226-03535-2 (paper)

To Charlotte,
who is life,
and love,
and *the reason*

Speech is civilization itself. The word, even the most contradictory word, preserves contact—it is silence which isolates.

Thomas Mann

When the fact has been accepted that African slaves were men and women like all other human beings, it is not difficult to imagine the depth of their fears, the agony of their anxieties, and the profundity of their griefs and sorrows when they were forcibly expatriated. We are fortunate in having a few personal accounts to confirm our empathy, written by some exceptional human beings who survived the experience, rose above it and left the legacy of their words.

St. Clair Drake

Words' meanings, but also the rhythm and syntax that frame and propel their concatenation, seek their culture as the final reference for what they are describing of the world. An A flat played twice on the same saxophone by two different men does not have to sound the same.

Amiri Baraka

Contents

Acknowledgments

I have often thought that "acknowledgments" represent a confession rather than an expression of gratitude. In them the author tries to atone for forcing his friends to battle with early drafts, half-realized outlines, and developing ideas. I know that mentioning the names of all those who have suffered on my behalf is scarcely enough. But I hope it provides some compensation for their fine generosity. Professors David Levin, Ralph Cohen, Jerry Ward, Michael Peinovich, Wole Soyinka, Hennig Cohen, Ezekiel Mphahlele, Alvin Aubert, Robert Hemenway, and Raymond Nelson all read portions of the manuscript. Their criticism and suggestions were of great value. Professors Arnold Rampersad and James Nash deserve special thanks since they usually serve as my "ideal readers"; when they are satisfied with my writing, I am sometimes able to relax. Mr. Robert Erwin was kind enough to read a group of my essays and to suggest that I might integrate them into a single discourse. Professor Barbara Herrnstein Smith acted as both friend and mentor as I labored to understand issues in linguistics and literary theory. The Center for Advanced Study in the Behavioral Sciences graciously invited me to join its roster of fellows for 1977–78, making available funds, secretarial and library assistance, and a magnificent environment in which to work. The National Endowment for the

Humanities also provided funds for 1977–78. The John Simon Guggenheim Memorial Foundation awarded me a fellowship for the 1979 academic year, freeing time for the completion of one section of the manuscript and for the revision of others. I am obviously indebted to all three institutions. A number of my colleagues at the Center read parts of the manuscript and offered sterling advice. I want to thank Professors Paul Sniderman, Alfonso Ortiz, Sidra Ezrahi, Carolyn Merchant, Alfred Kazin, and Sacvan Bercovitch for their magnanimity during the glorious Center year. I must also acknowledge my indebtedness to Kate Hughes, my secretary at the Center, who typed countless drafts of chapters with speed, accuracy, good humor, and keen editorial intelligence. My wife, Charlotte, was my most trusted friend, editor, and solace from the beginning to the end of this project. Our son, Mark, provided sane companionship for both of us during the process. Various journals and publishers granted permission to reprint material. I want to thank *Obsidian, Era, Minority Voices,* Edward Everett, Inc., and the Afro-American Studies Program of Brown University for their considerateness.

Faced with such a long list, I must conclude by acknowledging that those who aided me were flawless in their judgments and informed in their critiques. All mistakes and missteps in the present volume are, thus, my own: Mea Culpa.

Introduction

Scarcely more than a decade ago, a number of black spokesmen—including literary critics—assumed it was our turn to speak. The debate, indeed the larger conversation comprising American culture, had gone on too long without acknowledging black American voices. Our stance was nationalistic; our mode was frequently ahistorical; and our results were sometimes dreary. The familiar terms were "Black Aesthetic," "Black Power," "Nation Time," and so on. If this working vocabulary was limited, so, too, was our perspective. We assumed we were fighting for survival, and we took Malcolm X's words quite literally: we proceeded "by any means necessary."

When I talk with students and scholars today, I find that much of the work produced under the aegis of black nationalism is deemed the sound and fury of a troubled past. It need not be rehearsed, or reread, in our current, more sophisticated era. The present is an age of theory; the conversation has moved to another plane. I find such assertions unsettling, since they come from men and women situated at institutions that, fifteen years ago, would not have dreamed of admitting many of those who spoke for our rights and defended our dignity during the sixties and early seventies. I ask myself if there is always destined to be a protective insularity surrounding colleges and universities. To see life steadily and to see it whole is not an easy matter; the academy frequently seems ready to close debate before the task has even begun. Yet, I think those who are speaking from a perspective that was unavailable a few years back (for most black people, at any rate) are essentially correct. There has been a great deal of muddled thinking about black literature during the recent past. An obsessively nationalistic prospect is probably not the most fruitful approach to the black literary text. And it is, no doubt, time to move on to a more descriptively accurate and theoretically sophisticated level. In my own work, I have tried to follow the course suggested by these persuasions.

At the same time, I have neither ignored nor relinquished prerogatives gained—at great cost—during the past several years. If there is to be a transition from one universe of discourse to another, I would like to carry over the best that has been thought and said at earlier stages in the argument. If the pressing issues for scholars of black literature are no longer black revolution or building a strong black nation, what new concerns are to take their place? Surely the aim at this stage is not to toss all works of black literature into a general arena and see which emerge victorious. We have had enough battles royal.

A more appropriate response is a detailed description of the place occupied by works of black literature in black American culture. From such an account, one may proceed to an adequate explanation, or to theoretical insights. These efforts do not spring ab nihilo; they are considered valuable according to some scale of preferences. I assume they are always in the service of goals larger than the articulation of a set of theoretical propositions. The research in which I am currently engaged, for example, has as its end a method of analysis that will explain *how* black narrative texts written in English preserve and communicate culturally unique meanings. I am seeking a way—beyond verbal fiat—to substantiate a particular point of view on black American culture and art.

What follows in the present volume is an integration of several essays written during the past three years with some new formulations. The work is intended as a unit. It represents a portion of my attempt to describe the area in black American culture occupied by literary works of art. It returns to eighteenth-century black writers whom I dismissed out of hand during a more volatile stage of my career, treats salient issues in black culture, and provides an assessment of black literature and criticism from 1954 to 1976. It also looks to the future by offering some initial considerations for a specific theoretical approach to black American literature. The volume makes no pretense to a full literary or critical history of black America. It is, rather, a contribution to the larger conversation previously mentioned. It introduces selected topics in the study of black literature and criticism and dwells on them in what, I hope, are interesting ways. One cannot talk about everything in a single conversational turn, but one can at least aspire to be suggestive on the issues raised.

Since the text that follows represents a transitional effort, or the effort of an author in transition, I should note at the outset that I have relied on the findings of a number of disciplines in my attempt to arrive at an informed conception of black American literature and culture. I think it will be serviceable, therefore, if I establish a framework of concepts to guide the reader through some of the book's more technical passages. A traditional procedure is to situate such a framework in a first chapter and then develop the concepts that it sets forth in a sequence of carefully titled chapters. One problem with this procedure is that it calls undue attention to terminology and causes readers to infer the full nature of an author's claims before he has an opportunity to explore them. I have chosen this less obtrusive place to detail some theoretical notions that come to bear in my larger argument.

Culture, in my operative definition, is analagous to linguistic discourse.[1] A linguistic discourse is a structure consisting of language units higher than or "beyond" the sentence, i.e., two conjoined sentences, a myth, a folktale, a novel, and so on. Like all "structured" objects and processes, discourse is based on rules, principles, and conventional procedures. Its governing regularities are functions of the rules of language and language use in a particular society.

Prosodic features like pitch and stress, segmental elements such as phonemes, morphemes, and lexemes, and syntactic units all join in systematic ways to constitute any sentence or utterance. These sentences and utterances are, in turn, combined as coherent discourse by the rules and procedures that constitute the text-forming resources of a culture. Rules for the use of conjunctions and pronouns in English, for example, may be considered text-forming resources, and so, too, may the conventional procedures governing the recitation of, say, a "personal" narrative by a speaker engaged in conversation.

A useful analogy here is a game of chess.[2] The board, individual pieces, players, and moves comprise a "game of chess" only when they are set against a background (or upon a foundation) of systematic rules. In the most exacting sense, these rules make the observable acts and objects components of a game of chess and of no other game. Even an assiduous observer of two people playing chess could not provide a convincing or thorough explanation of what he was witnessing unless he had some knowledge of the rules.

Similarly, individuals who enter a culture where the language is unfamiliar may be capable (after a relatively brief period) of identifying and defining in their own terms any single word or sentence presented, and they may rapidly become adept at constructing interesting ethnographic accounts for their "home" cultures. But they will not comprehend the overall game of language, or the culture's composite of language games, until they have fully grasped the general rules and procedures of discourse operating within the culture. Their understanding will remain tenuous until they have engaged in the process that the symbolic anthropologist Clifford Geertz calls "thick description."[3]

Geertz employs the term to signify an investigator's attempt to unravel a culture's "multiplicity of complex conceptual structures, many of them superimposed upon or knotted into one another, which are at once strange, irregular, and inexplicit." In *The Interpretation of Cultures,* he makes it clear that a "conceptual structure" is a unit resulting from a culture's organization of the world. An "hour," an "inch," a "kilowatt," a "phoneme" (the minimal sound unit of a language) are all, in this sense, conceptual structures, or cultural units, whose patterning is a matter of systematic rules and codes. To return to our hypothetical game of chess, just as the knight's possible moves on the board are a key to the rules of the game, so one can say that a society's language (as a coded enterprise whose units express fundamental cultural concepts) plays a key role in any "thick description" of a culture. Geertz thus brings together linguistic discourse and cultural interpretation:

> We [anthropologists] are seeking in the widened sense of the term in which it encompasses very much more than talk, to converse with them [natives of a culture not one's own], a matter a great deal more difficult, and not only with strangers, than is commonly recognized . . . . Looked at in this way, the aim of anthropology is the enlargement of the universe of human discourse. [Pp. 13–14]

Surely this aim has been stated (at least once) for every conceivable discipline. But Geertz's use of a linguistic discourse model brings out what I consider basic similarities between literary analysis and cultural anthropology. In order to be convincing, research from both areas of scholarship must reveal an attention to the multiplicity of interrelated codes that give force to observable cultural phenomena. Both the literary and the cultural investigator must refuse simply to identify and define, in chauvinistic terms, the objects and events presented to view. Each must strive, instead, to *interpret* the manifestations of a culture in accordance with the unique, richly symbolic, and meaningful contexts within which such manifestations achieve their effects. The important word here is *context*, and once again an anthropologist—in this instance, Edmund Leach—offers an observation that helps to clarify my point of view:

> If you record unrehearsed conversation on tape you will find that on play-back very little of it is immediately comprehensible; yet, in context, all those present would have understood what was being said. This is because, in its original setting, the spoken utterance was only part of a larger whole. It had a

> metonymic (sign) relationship with everything else that was going on in the room at the same time, and the non-verbal "other" was also conveying part of the message.[4]

The statement emphasizes the importance of a communicative context in the interpretation of specifically linguistic cultural expressions.

In my larger argument, I use the foregoing notions of discourse, culture, and context in an attempt to reveal some of the underlying rules and conventional procedures of black American literature and culture. I begin with the assumption that the literary analyst must employ methods and materials from many disciplines in order to make sense of cultural expressions, or signs. A work of literature, for example, is a manifestation of the human capacity for symbolic behavior, and an entire field of anthropology is currently devoted to the study of men and women as agents who represent and transmit knowledge in symbolic form.[5] The literary work is also a form standing in a peculiar relationship to all other forms of verbal behavior in society. And the voluminous contemporary scholarship in the linguistic investigation of texts is one indication of the complexity of issues occasioned by this relationship.[6] Further, the process of reading a work of literature has, in recent years, been analyzed by psychologists, philosophers of language, and literary critical phenomenologists.[7] The result has been the appearance of "affective stylistics" and "implied readers" in the universe of discourse surrounding literature and verbal art. What I mean to suggest by this catalogue is the necessity, at the present time, of setting investigations of works of literature and verbal art in a framework that I call the "anthropology of art."[8] The phrase expresses for me the notion that art must be studied with an attention to the methods and findings of disciplines which enable one to address such concerns as the status of the artistic object, the relationship of art to other cultural systems, and the nature and function of artistic creation and perception in a given society.

In the present book, the "anthropology of art" signals an investigative strategy that I am striving to apply to black literature and culture. The black American poet and literary critic Larry Neal offered a reflection in one of his early essays that provides an additional sense of what this enterprise involves:

> Most western philosophical orientations have taken the force of meaning out of existence. . . . Let us take, for example, the disorientation one experiences when one sees a piece of African sculpture in a Madison Avenue art gallery. Ask yourself: What is it doing there? In Africa, the piece had ritual significance. It was a spiritual affirmation of the connection between man and his ancestors, and it implied a particular kind of ontology—a particular sense of being. . . . In the gallery or the salon it is merely an *objet d'art,* but for your [black Americans'] ancestors, it was a bridge between them and the spirit, a bridge between you and your soul in the progression of a spiritual lineage.[9]

What Neal suggests here is that an imaginative reconstruction of a cultural context is mandatory if one wishes to understand the meaning of the African sculpture. To offer a perspicacious and persuasive explanation of the work's discrete lines, planes, and angles would not be enough. And merely to subsume it under a general category such as "primitive art" might be disastrous for an effort to understand the sculpture as a cultural sign. Only an informed grasp—a "thick description"—of the interrelated codes of a particular African culture, Neal insists, can yield the authentic "force of meaning" of the work.[10]

The work that follows represents my attempt at cultural interpretation—my effort to converse within a particular tradition. By placing selected portions of text from the overall discourse of black American culture in an interdisciplinary perspective, I have tried to reveal the force of meaning of a culture and its literature. Though I have not succeeded entirely in removing the sculptures from the gallery (what Ishmael Reed calls "art detention centers"), I feel I have done a creditable job of arranging the gallery in ways that will give my readers a sense of Afro-American verbal art in context—in motion.

1 Terms for Order: Acculturation, Meaning, and the Early Record of the Journey

The object of black America's quest has always been the same—a meaningful set of what Kenneth Burke calls "terms for order."[1] The search for coherent arrangements of objects and events implies, at one level, the disruption of a prior unity, no matter how strained or tenuous. On a more abstract plane, it suggests a process existing on the far side of chaos. To understand our origins, we must journey through difficult straits. And in the end we may find only confusion. It is difficult, as Ralph Ellison demonstrates in *Invisible Man,* to conceive of encountering chaos without accompanying thoughts of one's own destruction. Most of us take refuge in the safe harbor of dreams, envisioning glorious years of the distant past or of the near future. Perhaps only poets, or writers confined to a situation that offers no alternatives, can and do make the effort at return.

The black writer, having attempted the journey, preserves details of his voyage in that most manifest and coherent of all cultural systems—language. Through his work we are allowed to witness, if not the trip itself, at least a representation of the voyage that provides some view of our emergence. This, I think, is what George Kent has in mind when he notes that *The Life of Olaudah Equiano or Gustavus Vassa the African Written by Himself* (1789) captures "the chaos swirling at the root of transplanted black life."[2]

Directing our attention to an early moment in the black past, Vassa writes:

> The first object which saluted my eyes when I arrived on the coast, was the sea, and a slave ship, which was then riding at anchor, and waiting for its cargo. These filled me with astonishment, which was soon converted into terror, when I was carried on board. I was immediately handled, and tossed up to see if I were sound, by some of the crew; and I was now persuaded that I had gotten into a world of bad spirits, and that they were going to kill me. Their complexions, too, differing so much from ours, their long hair, and the language they spoke (which was very different from any I had ever heard), united to confirm me in this belief.[3]

This succinct and powerful statement details the most rudimentary beginnings of black American literature and culture. Questions of origin are answered in the delineation of kidnaping and terror. The beginning is in victimization, and Vassa (to whom we shall return later) magnificently portrays what he calls "the adversity and variety of fortune" entailed by this condition.

Brought to the New World in chains, African captives could transport only certain parts of their traditional culture: customs, mores, and the deep, expressive components that provide the springs of creative genius. A number of scholars—including Melville Herskovits and W. E. B. Du Bois—have dealt with what are loosely called "African survivals in America."[4] Concentrating on patterns of community organization, religious worship, and even dress, these researchers have concluded that the African way of life was not terminated simply by a boat ride, as some scholars have charged.[5] Furthermore Du Bois, as well as contemporary writers such as John Blassingame, Paul Carter Harrison, and William D. Piersen, also notes the continuation of a more strictly defined African creativity.[6] Songs, dances, folktales, carvings on canes and flywhisks, and innumerable other manifestations indicate the persistence of a tradition deeply rooted in another continent.

Despite these carefully documented carryovers, however, there are early, self-conscious (written) products of the African imagination in America that reveal a vista of searching men and women caught between two worlds. The double nomenclature of Olaudah Equiano's (or Gustavus Vassa's) narrative serves as an emblem of this division. On the one hand, Africans were not free to be Africans; they found their traditional rituals and the instruments necessary for their performance suppressed by whites. On the other hand, they were defined by law as outsiders and were excluded from the free, human community that the Puritans designated a city of God in the New World. As slaves in perpetuity, as men and women deemed lower than animals, where could the first black Americans turn? What terms for order were available to them as they looked upon chaos?

One complex of attitudes and ideas readily at hand was orthodox Calvinism. Adopting the God of his white masters, the African captive could turn his face away from the miseries of oppression and think only of a divine realm. The first black poet to publish in America offers an example of this strategy. Jupiter Hammon was born a slave in 1711. His masters were members of the Lloyd family of Long Island. Biographical information on Hammon is scant, but he seems to have spent his entire life in service to one family. During the occupation of Long Island by British troops in the Revolutionary War, he lived in Hartford, Connecticut, and published at least one work there.[7] Apparently his owners were less oppressive than some slave owners, since he wrote, in "An Address to the Negroes of the State of New York" (1786), "I have great reason to be thankful that my lot has been so much better than most slaves have had. I suppose I have had more advantages and privileges than most of you who are slaves now have ever known, and I believe more than many white people have enjoyed, for which I desire to bless God, and pray that he may bless those who have given them to me."[8]

The tone of this passage characterizes the entire canon. Hammon's relationship to the world around him seems captured by the title of his dialogue, "The Kind Master and the Dutiful Servant" (c. 1783). Throughout his life, he pondered his duty to both his earthly and his heavenly master and spent more than a little time composing prose and verse recommending a similar course to fellow blacks. His connection with Africa—even by way of passing references—is tenuous indeed. He calls the slaves of New York "dear African brethren" at one instance in the "Address" cited above, and in a poem entitled "An Address to Miss Phillis Wheatley" (1778) he refers to the Boston poet's African origins:

Thou mightst been left behind
 Amidst a dark abode
God's tender mercy still combin'd
 Thou hast the holy word.[9]

The truth is, Hammon was not a man of this world. His work is most concerned with that day when the quick and the dead shall be judged. He conceived life sub specie aeternitatis, and thus mitigated the pain and difficulty of formulating, or seeking to fulfill, the obligations of a strictly secular role. His theme (for he had but one), therefore, fits the company of early white American efforts that devote exclusive attention to a teleological vision: "We live so little time in this world that it does not matter how wretched and miserable we are, if it prepares us for heaven. What is forty, fifty, or sixty years, when compared to eternity?" ("Address," p. 321). And it is precisely the shortness of earthly time moving toward the fullness of judgment that motivated Hammon to spend his own hours reading the Bible and contemplating heavenly things. His first published poem, "An Evening Thought, Salvation by Christ, with Penitential Cries" (1760), shows the result of these endeavors:

Ten Thousand Angels cry to Thee
Yea Louder than the Ocean.
Thou art the Lord, we plainly see;
Thou art the true Salvation.
Now is the Day, excepted Time:
The Day of Salvation;
Increase your Faith, do not repine;
Awake ye every nation.[10]

The work as a whole is an invocation of the final days; its

drama resides in the speaker's attempt to rise to the peak of celestial vision on the crude wings of doggerel verse. Twice he calls out in caesuric lines for the heavenly host to appear: "Come holy Spirit, Heavenly Dove" and "Come Blessed Jesus, Heavenly Dove." In other words, the poem is the poet's attempt to ring down the apocalypse.

If this was Hammon's first work, can it come as a surprise that his last contains the following? "But this [the quest for earthly liberty], my dear brethren, is by no means the greatest thing we have to be concerned about. Getting our liberty in this world, is nothing to our having the liberty of the children of God" ("Address," p. 319). There was hardly need for an individual who spent so much time in heaven to think of the demands of the tangible world in which he lived. The only reason Hammon championed education for blacks was that it would make the Bible accessible. The justification he gave for committed service to one's earthly master was that it might enable one to better one's lot through moral suasion based on biblical precedents. Moreover, if one had a "kind" master, one could follow him straight to heaven:

Master

My servant, Heaven is high above
Yea, higher than the sky:
I pray that God would grant his love,
Come follow me thereby.

Servant

Dear Master, now I'll follow thee
And trust upon the Lord;
The only safety that I see,
Is Jesus's holy word.[11]

At best, one can call Jupiter Hammon a committed Calvinist versifier. In seeking terms for order, he concluded that the "only safety" resided in total immersion in the word of Jesus as it is revealed by the Bible and as it must have been preached by the Protestant divines of Hartford, Connecticut, and of Queens Village, Long Island. The link with Africa seems severed in his canon, and there is little to recommend him to a secular world of war and death. Such a writer might justly have been employed by Harriet Beecher Stowe as a model for Uncle Tom. For Hammon, too, says he feels that earthly liberty is a state to be sought, but not by or for himself. The "younger negroes," as he phrases it, might profit by manumission, and the "white people" have shown the worth of liberty by their expenditures during the Revolutionary War ("Address," p. 219). But Hammon, a man advanced in years when he addressed his brothers in New York, was content to remain in bondage, granting little thought to his African homeland, giving his best efforts to a quest for heaven. His talents, like his thoughts, moved in a narrow channel, and it now seems he was capable of only the most unrefined verse and uninspiring prose. It was the appearance of Phillis Wheatley, marking a conceptualization by the black writer of a distinct role in America, that provided new terms for order.

When we move from Hammon's work to that of Wheatley, we leave behind the versifier to encounter the poet. We see the quill pen gracefully posed, suspended just above parchment. On the small writing table, an inkwell and a tiny closed volume further announce the subject's occupation. An arm is curved upward, left index finger resting pensively against the jaw. But if asked whether this is simply an ordinary eighteenth-century portrait of a writer at work, we would have to respond, no. For the inscription on the just-described frontispiece to *Poems on Various Subjects, Religious and Moral* (1773), reads: "Phillis Wheatley, Negro Servant to Mr. John Wheatley, of Boston." The picture strikes the informed consciousness as a singular—an almost revolutionary—signature on the scroll of American history. Like the stately robes and celestial backdrop of Raphaelle Peale's painting of the black Episcopal priest Absalom Jones (1810), the implements at Wheatley's table and her earnest concentration give the lie to that frequently repeated notion that all blacks (and especially those as far back in time as the eighteenth century) have perpetually spent their days in gross manual labor and their nights shuffling to the sound of exotic banjos.

Frontispiece to the 1773 edition of Phillis Wheatley's *Poems on Various Subjects, Religious and Moral* (photograph from the Moorland-Spingarn Research Center).

The primary biographical fact is that Phillis Wheatley was born in Africa and maintained a sense of her homeland throughout her life. In 1761, she arrived in America where, according to Margaretta Matilda Odell, one of her earliest biographers, the slave marketplace found her a "poor, naked child" and she was chosen as the peculiar purchase of the day by John and Susanna Wheatley. Mr. Wheatley was a successful Boston merchant, and his wife had expressed a desire to "obtain a young negress, with the view of training her up under her own eye, that she might, by gentle usage, secure herself a faithful domestic in her old age." So Phillis was taken home "in the chaise of her mistress."[12]

Most of the poet's critics have taken as a donnée the child's "culturelessness," a lack, it almost seems, of even the rudiments of humanity, such as language. It is possible (indeed, it is almost certain) that Wheatley, like thousands of other Africans kidnaped for the New World, spoke at least one African language, and perhaps a European pidgin, when first encountered by her purchasers. In any case, the Wheatleys' oldest daughter, Mary, was designated Phillis's tutor, and within sixteen months the child could read the most difficult parts of the Bible in English. And within a surprisingly brief time, the young African became certain that she possessed the muse's fire. She seems to have quickly reached the same conclusion as Dr. Johnson's Imlac: "Being now resolved to be a poet, I saw every thing with a new purpose; my sphere of attention was suddenly magnified: no kind of knowledge was to be overlooked."

It is virtually impossible, then, to regard the portrait forming the frontispiece as a drawing of a common black subject. And at first glance, it is difficult for a reader to understand why Wheatley fell victim to the following censorious critique from one of her white contemporaries: "Religion has produced a Phyllis Whately [*sic*]; but it could not produce a poet. The compositions published under her name are below the dignity of criticism. The heroes of the Dunciad are to her, as Hercules to the author of that poem."[13] We shall take up the motivating factors for this pronouncement, which happens to be by Thomas Jefferson, later. For the moment, one might note that in the frontispiece there are already lines of verse on the parchment. And while they are indecipherable, today's reader has an ample Wheatley canon and can, perhaps, arrive at a fairer judgment than Jefferson's. In his monograph *Phillis Wheatley in the Black American Beginnings,* William Robinson concludes that Wheatley wrote over one hundred poems during her brief career.[14] If one considers that a number of these efforts were several pages long, one promptly discards the notion that the poet's work is too "slight" to require attention.

The barriers to a just evaluation, however, are enormous. Wheatley's life and work have for decades formed an essential part of a controversy surrounding the intellectual and imaginative abilities of Africans. Jefferson's remarks may have set the chorus off, but its echo was heard as far away as Europe.[15] And the debate concerning Wheatley's intellectual virtues and limitations has extended to our own century. Vernon Loggins, in *The Negro Author in America,* says:

> Although there can at the present day be little emotional response to her poems, there is justly enough the greatest curiosity over the manner in which she composed them. The facility and thoroughness with which she, a slave transported from Africa, imitated the artful idiom of Alexander Pope and his meticulous school while she was still scarcely more than a child presents one of those marvels of precocity which baffle psychological explanation.[16]

And Amiri Baraka (né LeRoi Jones), one of the most influential spokesmen of the past decade, has condemned Wheatley for her failure to "get down" and off-beat in the manner of southern field slaves, who punctuated the pinewood air with anguished shouts and hollers.[17] In a later chapter I shall attempt to discover some of the governing principles of such criticism. Here I shall try to set forth an informed view of Wheatley, based on the poetical canon itself.

In the 21 December 1767 issue of the *Newport* (Rhode Island) *Mercury* there appeared "On Messrs. Hussey and Coffin," Wheatley's first poem.

Did Fear and Danger so perplex your Mind,
As made you fearful of the whistling Wind?
Was it not Boreas knit his angry Brows
Against you? or did consideration bow?
To lend you Aid, did not his Winds combine?
To stop your passage with a churlish Line,
Did haughty Eolus with Contempt look down
With aspect windy, and a study'd Frown?
Regard them not:—The Great Supreme, the Wise
Intends for something hidden from our Eyes . . . .[18]

A career was launched, and it is interesting to note how the boundaries of the poet's canon are set in this early work. The classical pagan is juxtaposed with the omnipresent Christian. The raging sea, all nature's forces, are powerless before the "Great Supreme." And what if the honorable Hussey and Coffin had, by some ill chance, been "snatch'd away" by the "groundless Gulph"? The poet's answer is that their souls would have soared to heaven through the only grace mortals may know—that of a radiant God.

The poem, however, is more than a simple paean. Toward its conclusion, the poet grows increasingly conscious of her own role: *"Had I the Tongue of a Seraphim, how would I exalt thy / Praise: thy Name as incense to the Heavens should fly."*[19] The didacticism of the poem's beginning couplets and the search for high inspiration that comes at the work's ending show that Wheatley had seized for herself a place among those who claimed poetry as their particular "calling," an important word in the vocabulary of American Puritanism. Before their first voyage out to fulfill an errand in the wilderness, John Cotton told the Pilgrims:

> Faith drawes the heart of a Christian to live in some warrantable calling; as soon as ever a man begins to looke towards God, and the wayes of his grace, he will not rest, till he finds out some warrantable Calling and imployment . . . . A Christian would no sooner have his sinne pardoned, then his estate to be settled in some good calling, though not as a mercenary slave, but he would offer it up to God as a free-will Offering, he would have his condition and heart settled in Gods peace, but

> his life settled in a good calling, though it be but of a day-labourer, yet make me as one that may doe thee some service.[20]

Cotton's prerequisites for a "warrantable" calling were that it serve the public good, that it be a God-given gift, and that it be easy of access. All three were perfectly in harmony with Doctor Johnson's stipulations on the general character of a poet.

It is a reassuring fact, in light of Wheatley's choice of a calling, that she produced far better poems than "On Messrs. Hussey and Coffin." In 1768 she wrote "To the University of Cambridge, in New England." Although the poem is the work of a seventeen-year-old black servant, its versification reads like that of an assured aristocrat:

> Students, to you 'tis giv'n to scan the heights
> Above, to transverse the ethereal space,
> And mark the systems of revolving worlds.
> . . . .
> Improve your privileges while they stay,
> Ye pupils, and each hour redeem, that bears
> Or good or bad report of you to heav'n.
> Let sin, that baneful evil to the soul,
> By you be shunn'd, nor once remit your guard.[21]

The passage has the tone of a parent chiding a son or daughter off to university. But later the speaker identifies herself as an "Ethiop," and our critical interest grows. Why? Because such a word, such smoothly flowing verse suggest not only the thoroughness with which Wheatley had learned her craft, but also the tensions inherent for her in the poetical calling.

One pauses to ask if her reference to nationality was calculated merely to win added admiration from or to shock a white public that sometimes argued that the human heartbeat is not a property of the black world, or whether it is actually an indication of an extended African consciousness. Here one can look to Umberto Eco's *A Theory of Semiotics.*[22] *Ethiop* as a sign-vehicle is governed by two functives—content and expression. What Eco specifies as the content-plane, however, is not a simple dictionary definition, but rather what he calls the "encyclopedia"—an area that is more like a detailed map than a series of discrete dictionary entries. An analyst of Wheatley's verse can speak either of the multiple "connotations" of *Ethiop* or, more exactly, of the complex mappings of the term's content. And it seems to me that the most persuasive mapping for the term, as it is employed by the poet, moves in the direction of an extended African consciousness.

Beyond all else, as I have stated, Wheatley conceived of herself as a poet. The qualifying marker which now must be added is *African*. Although Richard Wright states in "The Literature of the Negro in the United States" that Wheatley was a black writer who moved in harmony with the larger culture of white America,[23] I feel that the poet remained both outside and above the general culture of her age. Rather than a firm conception of her Americanness—something unavailable to most occupants of North America before the 1780s—Wheatley felt she had a peculiarly African gift to contribute to an era of turbulance and sudden mortality. In the still somewhat primitive confines of eighteenth-century New England, she allowed her imagination to wander over classical fields, to soar to empyreal heights, to dwell in the realms of recollection, and to venture beyond the grave's seal to the domain of death. I would suggest, therefore, that the real impetus for her verse was her felt sense of her own unique stature among a creative company:

> The happier *Terence** all the choir inspir'd
> His soul replenish'd and his bosom fir'd
> But say, ye *Muses,* why this partial grace,
> to one alone of *Afric's* sable race;
> From age to age transmitting thus his name
> With the first glory in the rolls of fame?
>
> [*Poems,* p. 4]

Wheatley placed an asterisk after "Terence," and the footnote reads: "He was an African by birth." Significantly, the poem in which the above lines appear is the dedicatory work in *Poems on Various Subjects, Religious and Moral,* Wheatley's only published volume. Thus the poet addresses her readers from the outset as one intent on expanding the African component of the rolls of fame to include her own name. The designation *Ethiop* thus has a firm grounding. And the advice tendered to Harvard students at the conclusion of "To the University of Cambridge" takes on new dimensions:

> Ye blooming plants of human race devine,
> An *Ethiop* tells you 'tis your greatest foe [sin],
> Its transient sweetness turns to endless pain,
> And in immense perdition sinks the soul.
>
> [*Poems,* p. 6]

This is heady indeed from one who "not long since" had left "the land of errors, and the Egyptian gloom."

Wheatley clearly seems to have considered herself an exception to the common run. The reasons for this included her Africanness and her strong, partially Christian conviction of the poet's importance in human affairs. In combination with these, she shared those wonderful eighteenth-century views of Africa as a land of noble savages. Chronological primitivism has full sway in her reply to a Gentleman of the Navy, where Africa is depicted as follows:

> . . . pleasing Gambia on my soul returns,
> With native grace in spring's luxuriant reign,
> Smiles the gay mead, and Eden blooms again,
> The various bower, the tuneful flowing stream
> The soft retreats, the lovers golden dream,
> Her soil spontaneous, yields exhaustless stores.
>
> [*Poems,* p. 86]

The notion of a talented and uncorrupted noble savage was very much a part of the century in which Wheatley lived. And when the poet, for health reasons, traveled to England in the 1770s, this notion surely accounted for more than a modicum of the curiosity that surrounded her presence and poetry among the British. She joined the gallery occupied during the same century by Stephen Duck, Robert Burns, and others. Nonetheless, she was treated kindly while abroad and may even have had an opportunity to oversee part of the production of her first volume by "A. Bell, bookseller."[24]

At Mrs. Wheatley's urging, Phillis returned to America in July of 1773. Her mistress's health was rapidly failing, and the receipt of early copies of *Poems on Various Subjects* and the author's attempts to publicize and distribute the volume in America (where it saw a first edition in 1786) were clouded by Susanna's death on 3 March 1774. During the years 1774 to 1778, Phillis seems to have produced enough new work to warrant a 1779 announcement in the *Boston Evening Post and General Advertiser* of a second volume of her poetry. The work was never released, however, since it would have been difficult for even the most committed bibliophile during the pinched days of the Revolutionary War to think of paying twelve pounds for a leather-bound edition of the projected three-hundred-page volume.

During the last years of her life, Wheatley seems to have moved from one locale to another, sometimes in the company of her husband, John Peters, whom she married in 1778, but more often, it seems, alone. According to biographers, these years from 1778 to 1784 were ones of poverty and recurring bouts of the severe asthma that had troubled her since youth. She gave birth to three children, all of whom died in infancy. Her own death came on 5 December 1784.

Although during the thirty years after the first publication of *Poems on Various Subjects* at least seven American editions appeared, and although complete editions or substantial groupings of her poems have appeared between 1835 and the present, Wheatley remains virtually unrecognized as a poet. One reason is the complex array of factors that must be segmented and classified in advance of precise judgment. Nonetheless, I think it is fair to say that the poet's work is at least sui generis. It proceeds from one with a strong sense of African identity. At the same time, it reveals all the putative generality of the committed Augustan writer. Like the cold pastoral of a later, English, creator, it teases us out of thought, forcing us to ponder what "manner" of people could find itself enslaved by fortune and yet produce a poet who dared describe the universe. At times Wheatley's verse is tight and cramped in its heroic couplets—those balanced objectifications of a world view according to which the cosmos was subject to reason. If Wheatley does not satisfy those who wonder at her seeming obliviousness to the condition of the vast, dark body, seven-hundred-thousand strong, held slaves in perpetuity, perhaps it is because these commentators have failed to survey the poet's life, work, and society as complex, interrelated phenomena. The most just assessment seems to be that Wheatley's canon ranks with the best that early America has to offer.

The Africanness, the Christian import, and the creative self-consciousness that combine to form a discernible pattern in Wheatley's canon are more than matched in the work of Gustavus Vassa. To judge by the time span between Hammon's "An Evening Thought" and *The Life of Olaudah Equiano*, early black American literature developed with amazing rapidity, leaving behind the devout otherworldliness of its first published author and in just thirty years bringing forth an assured, at times brilliant, treatment of the secular problems of Africans in an alien world. Gustavus Vassa's narrative begins with a description of Essaka, a village in Benin (now Nigeria), where the author was born in 1745. Life in the village, where all men and women are chaste and free, serves as a referent for the author throughout his account. Against Essaka's seemly backdrop are set the brutality of the European slave trade, the horrors of West Indian slavery, the changing fortunes of the Seven Years' War between England and France, the cunning mechanics of the eighteenth-century industrial revolution, and the various competing theologies of a world in transition. As one might gather from the foregoing, the narrator sets forth myriad experiences, but he always remains the "African" specified by the work's title, one upon whom "all the adversity and variety of fortune . . . served only to rivet and record" the manner and customs of his homeland.

It is not Vassa's love of country alone that provided a unifying cast for the work. There is a subtlety in the *Life* that defies the single view. For it contains certain collocations of words, or "foregroundings," that do not easily yield their meanings to the casual reader. The Russian formalists were the first to introduce the concept of "foregrounding" to describe an instance in literary works where an unusual grouping of words calls attention to itself. In more recent years, Geoffrey Leech has employed the concept in interpreting Dylan Thomas and has also used the phrase, "cohesion of foregrounding," to describe the repetition of certain foregroundings within a single text.[25] What I am suggesting in the case of Vassa is that foregroundings and their cohesion provide a certain force of meaning in the narrative.

The deeper semantic aspects of the book are seen in the narrator's progressive ease in the company of his "new" countrymen (the British), his omnipresent urge to enjoy the rights and privileges of a free man, his growing comprehension of the industrial revolution, and his expanding awareness of the true path to Christian salvation. What one has is a sophisticated developmental autobiography. The only way to take it as the episodic rambling of an exotic primitive is to fail to provide an adequate code to contain the work's elusive possibilities. For only at a very primitive level of literary understanding could one interpret Vassa's assertions of the "unbounded credulity and superstition" of his fellow Essakans and his descriptions of the indigenous purity of Africa's interior as testimony from the school of noble savagery.

A consideration of one of the *Life*'s more striking foregroundings lends support to a claim for the work as a carefully crafted aesthetic text. Vassa says of his long journey with his kidnapers to the west coast of Africa: "I saw no mechanics whatever in all the way. . . . The chief employment in all these countries was agriculture, and both the males and females, as with us, were brought up to it, and trained in the arts of war" (*Life,* p. 27). His first encounter with machine culture is aboard the *African Snow,* the slave ship that carried him to the West Indies. On board, he is amazed by the quadrant and by all other aspects of navigation. But in one of those vivid verbal structures so prevalent in the *Life,* Vassa—who is almost the only black on a Virginia plantation—captures one of the most significant implications of the European industrial revolution:

> I was one day sent for to his [the master's] dwelling house to fan him; when I came into the room where he was I was very much affrighted at some things I saw, and the more so as I had seen a black woman slave as I came through the house, who was cooking the dinner, and the poor creature was cruelly loaded with various kinds of iron machines; she had one particularly on her head, which locked her mouth so fast that she could scarcely speak and could not eat or drink. I was astonished and shocked at this contrivance, which I afterwards learned was called the iron muzzle. [*Life*, p. 34]

Not only has he arrived in a land moving toward a new mechanical order (one in which the African is muzzled and cut off from nourishment), but also he has come face to face with a culture where objects of manufacture are put to cruel and inhumane use.

These conclusions are hinted in the first chapter of the *Life* when the author notes that the Africans' desire for products of industry (e.g., firearms) often occasioned intertribal wars designed to procure slaves as objects of barter in the transatlantic slave trade. The narrator's final response, however, is not to advocate casting out technology. Instead, he urges the conversion of technology to a more salutary end. Near the conclusion of his narrative, he asserts that various articles of "usefulness" are the "pleasing substitutes for the *torturing thumbscrew,* and the *galling chain*" (*Life*, p. 190). Those who will welcome such a shift are none other than British industralists. It is they who recognize the desirability of ending the slave trade and engaging Africa as a source of raw materials and a market for commerce.

From a bemused, frightened child overwhelmed by machines, the narrator moves to a stance as a prophet for a new commercial-industrial utopia in which England and Africa play complementary roles. Of course, such a projection and the way in which it is reached in the *Life* do not simply manifest Vassa's skill at foregrounding. They also reveal a stunning awareness of eighteenth-century economic and political currents. British industrialists did, finally, exert a large influence in the abolition of the slave trade, and they certainly had very fixed notions about the "civilizing" effects of commerce on the peoples of the world.

There are other unusual groupings of words and episodes that illustrate the depth and complexity of the *Life*. They surround the narrator's experiences with the sea, mercantilism, and religion as ordering constructs in a variegated existence. By careful juxtapositions (e.g., Christian baptism and a nearly fatal plunge into the Thames),[26] seemingly naive disclaimers, and an artful blend of simple narration and forceful exposition, Vassa shows that it is possible for an African to become a complete, gentle Christian and a learned abolitionist. For if there is a public voice in the *Life,* it is one that ceaselessly condemns the abuses of slavery and seeks to justify the equality of Africans, while revealing, at the same instant, the author's own personal sense of salvation and freedom in a manifold world. In sum, the work amply satisfies the expectations set forth by its demurring author: "If, then, the following narrative does not appear sufficiently interesting to engage general attention, let my motive be some excuse for its publication . . . . If it affords any satisfaction to my numerous friends, at whose request it has been written, or in the smallest degree promotes the interest of humanity, the ends for which it was undertaken will be fully attained, and every wish of my heart gratified" (*Life,* p. 4). Not only did Vassa promote the interests of humanity, but he also provided an enthralling narration of terms for order that subsequent African writers in America have adopted. His adamant call for black liberation and his repeated speculations that Africans are the chosen people of the Lord combine to give the *Life* a peculiarly modern tenor. It stands well in a line of accomplished successors.

The assumption that the representation of eighteenth-century black American literature and culture given in the work of Hammon, Wheatley, and Vassa is complete would be unwarrented. Dorothy Porter's six-hundred-fifty-page collection, *Early Negro Writing, 1760–1837,* is enough to forestall such an assumption.[27] And yet, one can suggest that broad designs and early patterns in black life and creativity are elucidated by the three authors treated here. What emerges is the picture of a complex eighteenth-century situation and a complex black response to it.

On a first view, "acculturation" seems to explain everything: Hammon's progress toward Christian orthodoxy, Wheatley's engagement with the God and muses of her white overlords, Vassa's detailing (in Pepysian fashion) of his education as a gentleman. Such acts—and their representation in literature—demonstrate the urge to move into the larger current of life in a slaveholding society. Wheatley's reverence, in other words, seems a genuine High Church piety. Hammon's overweening counsels of forbearance do not appear to be charades. And Vassa is monumentally pleased with his achievement in the arts of a refined civilization.

At what level, then, is one justified in considering the works of these authors apart from a general content nebula called "Western culture"? The answer resides in the nature of any cultural phenomenon considered under the aspect of "acculturation." Such phenomena always entail manifold tensions. There are always competing systems of meanings. In the American example, the polarity between Africans and whites was sharp from the beginning and became more acute through the implausible (but, nevertheless, determined) efforts made by many of the country's keenest minds to set culture where "nature" would not relent. The black person always carried as referents a land of ideal civilization called Africa and an imperium in imperio filled with tangible men and accomplishments called black America. He thus refused to become merely an animal in nature. Nor would he consent to be a silent cog in white industrial machines.

Instead, black Americans insisted on the privileged status of their own semantic fields, those abstract domains in which certain basic units had properties quite different from those that the larger culture tried to encode. For example, / Africa / was an 《ideal homeland》. Again, / Christianity / was a 《comfort against life's uncertainties》.[28] And what could have been more precarious and indeterminate than the life of Africans in eighteenth-century America? In extending the notion of distinctive black American lexical and conceptual fields, one might turn to an analogy employed by John Lyons in his discussion of field theory in semantics:

> What are generally considered to be different dialects of the same language may differ, often quite considerably, in phonology and grammar; and in this respect they are different language systems. But there will be a greater or less degree of regular correspondence between the forms of one dialect and the forms of another; and it is by virtue of the recognition of this correspondence that speakers of different dialects can understand one another (to the extent that they can) and will say that they use many of the same words, but pronounce them differently.[29]

In the present discussion of competing meanings in the acculturation process, what I am suggesting is that there must certainly be a degree of regular correspondence between behavioral forms (including, of course, linguistic forms) if two cultures are to coexist. On the other hand, these correspondences should not obscure the fact that an analyst of the acculturation process is faced with differing behavioral *systems*. The black American's conceptual field (what some semanticists call the area of "sense" or *Sinnfeld*), it seems to me, must have differed considerably in its systematic organization from that of his white American master, enslaver, owner, or coinhabitant of the American landscape. Though there was surely a regular correspondence between the lexical field (what some semanticists call the *Wortfeld*) of the white and that of the black American that made communication possible, it seems logical that blacks would not subconsciously (and certainly not consciously) have modified their conceptual field to reflect the white American "sense" of lexical items such as *night, dark, black, evil, death*. It seems unlikely as well that black Americans adopted the conceptualization of the word *Africa* that underlay the white person's employment of the term. If such a shift in conceptualization had occurred, it seems quite illogical that blacks would have continued to designate some of their most prized institutions in America as "African." The question that is always at issue in cases of acculturation, I think, is the nature of the reality undergirding materializations of the cultures (again, including linguistic forms) that are beginning to intersect. When I spoke above, for example, of the refusal of nature to relent, I might have said that there are certain structures in the external world (such as classes of natural, biological kinds) that are independent of lexical items, that do not rely for their behavioral similarities on that great distinguisher of culture—language. Despite the attempts of white Americans to promote a phenotypic difference (the pigmentation of black Americans) into a difference *in kind,* blacks had but to look to the world of nature in order to see the absurdity of this attempt. The semantic fields of the black American would have continued, it seems to me, to reflect a specifically black American segmentation and classification of experience.

And the related sets of words and concepts for eighteenth-century blacks did, in fact, stand in systematic opposition to a white American ordering of "reality." A neighboring lexical item for *Africa* for many blacks during the eighteenth century, for example, was *home*. Moreover, at a collocational level of language—on a plane, that is, where words come together to form meaningful constructs—phrases such as "intelligent black *man*" and "beautiful black *woman*" were semantic anomalies for many of the most talented white minds of the century. One might argue, therefore, that black Americans preserved their own concepts of experience despite the pressures of acculturation. One might additionally argue that blacks were able, as a result, to introduce into the total *Sinnfeld* new dimensions of experience.

At best, acculturation must be viewed as a dynamic process, one in which meanings overlapped, conflicted, vied with one another for ascendency. This dynamism is cogently represented in black literature in the functional oppositions seen in various verbal structures, for example, the two names in Vassa's title—one African and one English. Or the "Ethiop" providing moral guidance for "blooming plants of human race devine." In Hammon, one sees the dichotomy between the desires of an "old" African and the legitimate volitions of younger ones. In black literary texts, such oppositions are often systematic. Hence they cannot always be categorized as random instances of "irony." In Vassa's work, for example, the foregroundings are cohesive and allow the reader to grasp the various tensions of the narrator's cultural situation. The turbulent West Indian tides stand in contrast to the calm ports of England; the harmonious, pastoral world of Essaka is opposed to the chaotic arena of the French and English wars; the narrator's ignorance of English is in sharp contrast to his verbal facility as a diplomat, epistler, and author. The specific terms employed in these oppositional units are not the most important elements. What is significant is the relationship that exists between them.[30] For it is, finally, the nature of the connections that serves to elucidate the structure of the texts and, perhaps, the world view from which they spring. Black literary texts, therefore, offer a representation of experience in ways that suggest to the reader a unique situation and a distinctive realm of signification.

Still, one cannot deny claims that early black writers moved in harmony with their era, from an all-consuming Christian spirituality to a conception of the writer's role as political spokesman (e.g., the abolitionism of Vassa). From borrowed celestial terms, black writers progressed to a detailing of pragmatic, secular conditions that demand the writer's attention. If one can logically believe that Hammon, Wheatley, and Vassa looked upon chaos, one can be assured on investigating their writings that they were not struck dumb by it.

The details of the journey back are perserved and articulated in the black text. And these early terms for order might be characterized by a quatrain from the Caribbean poet Tony McNeill:

> Missed by my maps,
> still compassed by reason,
> my ship sails, coolly, between
> Africa and heaven.[31]

The poles here are idealizations, but the middle distance is secular, "compassed by reason." And it is precisely this middle ground that the black writer had to travel. Once he was on the shores of the New World, both Africa and heaven became green lights at the ends of faraway docks.

If whites were uncertain before the "freeman," the "free person of color," their uncertainty did not spring from the abstract space designated by *free*. It resulted (as I have suggested above) from the area constituted by *man* or *person*. The clearest marker here, I think, is language, a palpable outgrowth of reason. The effort to project one's voice over an undifferentiated black mass becomes difficult when whites hear forceful, perhaps contradictory, voices in return. When Caliban does not curse, but speaks in eloquent rational terms about his own situation, it is virtually impossible to ignore his distinctive, *human* presence.

One response is to purge the island, to send him away. The first meeting of the American Colonization Society (25 December 1816) was held slightly more than a quarter century after the publication of Vassa's narrative. The motive of the society was to provide an alternative residence for America's free people of color. If they were sent to Africa, the society argued, blacks would not only be better off, but they could also serve as pioneers for a new dawn of African civilization. They could become missionaries of God, culture, and commerce—an advance guard among the infidel. But for all the society's sweet reasonableness, there were those blacks who took issue. On 24 January 1817 came the equal but opposite voice of the freeman, issuing from the city that had witnessed the signing into being of the United States itself:

> Relieved from the miseries of slavery, many of us by your aid, possessing the benefits which industry and integrity in this prosperous country assure to all its inhabitants, enjoying the rich blessings of religion, by opportunities of worshipping the only true God, under the light of Christianity, each of us according to his understanding; and having afforded to us and to our children the means of education and improvement; we have no wish to separate from our present homes, for any purpose whatsoever. Contented with our present situation

> and condition, we are not desirous of increasing their prosperity but by honest efforts, and by the use of those opportunities for their improvement, which the constitution and laws allow to all. It is, therefore, with painful solicitude, and sorrowing regret, we have seen a plan for colonizing the free people of color of the United States on the coast of Africa, brought forward under the auspices and sanction of gentlemen whose names give value to all they recommend, and who certainly are among the wisest, the best, and the most benevolent of men, in this great nation. If the plan of colonizing is intended for our benefit, and those who now promote it will never seek our injury, we humbly and respectfully urge, that it is not asked for by us: nor will it be required by any circumstances, in our present or future condition, as long as we shall be permitted to share the protection of excellent laws and just government which we now enjoy, in common, with every individual of the community.[32]

For today's reader, these seemingly humble, gentle, polite (even entertaining) words may be translated: "Hell, no! We won't go!" James Forten, a veteran of the Revolutionary War and a man who later aided the financing of William Loyd Garrison's *Liberator,* is the author, but the sentiments expressed were general enough to instill a sense of community in free blacks throughout America.[33] The temporal middle distance was "home."

One means of preserving this American home was through acts of speech and writing. Anticolonization among blacks led to convention orations and resolutions, to the founding of newspapers like *Freedom's Journal* (1827), and to the abolitionist movement, ignited in Boston by David Walker's fiery *Appeal to the Coloured Citizens of the World* (1829). And in Forten's letter there is no lack of concern for "a portion of our brethren who are now held in slavery in the south."[34] If colonization becomes a reality, family ties will be broken between those who emigrate and those who remain in bondage. The greater threat, though, is the disappearance of "the voice of the suffering sons of Africa":

> To those of our brothers who shall be left behind, there will be assured perpetual slavery and augmented sufferings. Diminished in numbers, the slave population of the southern

> states, which by its magnitude alarms its proprietors, will be easily secured. Those among their bondsmen who feel that they should be free, by rights which all mankind have from God and nature, and who thus may become dangerous to the quiet of their masters, will be sent to the colony; and the tame and submissive will be retained, and subjected to increased rigor.[35]

The epistle is as much *about* language as it is *in* language. It possesses, one might say, a certain linguistic monumentality in its oppositions—to go or to stay, to speak or to remain silent—and provides an expanded set of terms for order. It mentions "arts," "habits of industry," "foresight," and the "rich blessings of the only true God." But the cardinal consideration, I believe, is that the address, as a document in words, exists. It provides a rationale for resisting the designs of those whites who desired silence.

Forten is aware of the virtues of "opportunities for instruction and improvement" among blacks. But he is careful to speak of such "opportunities" as being ex post facto phenomena which occur only when slaves are "by degrees relieved from bondage."[36] The "instruction" of slaves was a risky enterprise in southern states; it was expressly forbidden by law in most. The fact that the author of the address details the possibility of slaves' becoming a threat to their master's "quiet," however, shows how finely the document is tuned. Surely, those blacks who "feel that they should be free" will eventually add their voices to the general chorus and contribute to the mapping of the American ground on which the author and others were determined to remain.

In the southern states, there seemed to exist only a musical chorus—"caroling softly" the "souls of slavery." Spirituals, work songs, and field shouts and hollers (like those Baraka wanted Wheatley to imitate, even at a remove of several hundred miles)—these were the expressive black modes. Or so said white commentators in the countless novels of the Plantation Tradition.[37] It was all one big strum on the old banjo. Song, to be sure, has its own resonant importance in the black past. The texts of spirituals, ballads, chants, and so forth, can unlock vast stores of meanings. But here it is a more unitary voice that is of interest. Where was the articulate Caliban whom Forten saw troubling the master's calm? Part of the answer has already been provided: both Wheatley and Vassa were slaves. But they were of the North or, finally, of America's great parent country, England. Even though Wheatley's canon demonstrates in so many subtle ways that she preserved a sense of Africa in the New World, her work could scarcely serve as a model for southern bondsmen who shared few of her privileges. *The Life of Olaudah Equiano,* by contrast, was prototypical for the black voice that emerged from the prison-house of American slavery.

2 *Autobiographical Acts and the Voice of the Southern Slave*

The southern slave's struggle for terms for order is recorded by the single, existential voice engaged in what Elizabeth Bruss calls "autobiographical acts."[1] How reliable are such acts? Benedetto Croce called autobiography "a by-product of an egotism and a self-consciousness which achieve nothing but to render obvious their own futility and should be left to die of it." And a recent scholar of black autobiography expresses essentially the same reservations: "Admittedly, the autobiography has limitations as a vehicle of truth. Although so long an accepted technique towards understanding, the self-portrait often tends to be formal and posed, idealized or purposely exaggerated. The author is bound by his organized self. Even if he wishes, he is unable to remember the whole story or to interpret the complete experience."[2] A number of eighteenth-and nineteenth-century American thinkers would have taken issue with these observations. Egotism, self-consciousness, and a deep and abiding concern with the individual are at the forefront of American intellectual traditions, and the formal limitations of autobiography were not of great concern to those white authors who felt all existent literary forms were inadequate for representing their unique experiences. The question of the autobiography's adequacy, therefore, entails questions directed not only toward the black voice in the

South, but also toward the larger context of the American experiment as a whole.

Envisioning themselves as God's elect and imbued with a sense of purpose, the Puritans braved the Atlantic on a mission into the wilderness. The emptiness of the New World, the absence of established institutions and traditions, reinforced their inclination to follow the example of their European forebears and brothers in God. They turned inward for reassurance and guidance. Self-examination became the sine qua non in a world where some were predestined for temporal leadership and eventual heavenly reward and others for a wretched earthly existence followed by the fires of hell. The diary, the journal, the meditation, the book of evidences drawn from personal experiences were the literary results of this preoccupation with self, and even documents motivated by religious controversy often took the form of apology or self-justification. A statement from Jonathan Edwards's *Personal Narrative* offers a view of this tradition: "I spent most of my time in thinking of divine things, year after year: often walking alone in the woods, and solitary places, for meditation, soliloquy, and prayer, and converse with God; and it was always my manner at such time, to sing forth my contemplations."[3]

The man alone, seeking self-definition and salvation, certain that he has a God-given duty to perform, is one image of the white American writer. Commenting on Edwards and the inevitable growth of autobiography in a land without a fully articulated social framework, Robert Sayre writes: "Edwards could and had to seek self-discovery within himself because there were so few avenues to it outside himself. The loneliness and the need for new forms really go together. They are consequences of one another and serve jointly as inducements and as difficulties to autobiography."[4] This judgment must be qualified, since Edwards's form does not differ substantially from John Bunyan's, and his isolated meditations fit neatly into a Calvinistic spectrum, but Sayre is fundamentally correct when he specifies a concern with solitude and a desire for unique literary expression as key facets of the larger American experience.

Despite the impression of loneliness left by Edwards and the sense of a barren and unpromising land for literature left by comments like those of Hawthorne in his preface to *The Marble Faun* or James in *Hawthorne*, there were a number of a priori assumptions available to the white American thinker. They developed over a wide chronological span (the original religious ideals becoming, like those treated in the discussion of black writers above, increasingly secular) and provided a background ready to hand. There was the white writer's sense that he was part of a new cultural experience, that he had gotten away from what D. H. Lawrence calls his old masters and could establish a new and fruitful way of life in America. There was the whole panoply of spiritual sanctions; as one of the chosen people, he was responsible for the construction of a new earthly paradise, one that would serve as a holy paradigm for the rest of the world. There was the white writer's belief, growing out of the liberal, secular thought of Descartes, Locke, and Newton, that the individual was unequivocally responsible for his own actions; a man was endowed with inalienable rights, and one of these was the right to educate himself and strive for commercial success. There was also the feeling that America offered boundless opportunities for creative originality: a unique culture with peculiar sanctions should produce a sui generis art.

Thus, while James's "extraordinary blankness—a curious paleness of colour and paucity of detail" was characteristic for some early white Americans, there were also more substantial aspects or qualities of the American experience that stood in contrast to this "blankness." The writer could look to a Puritan ontology and sense of mission, to conceptions of the self-made man, or to a prevailing American concern for unique aesthetic texts as preshaping influences for his work. The objective world provided both philosophical and ideological justifications for his task. When Emerson wrote, "Dante's praise is that he dared to write his autobiography in colossal cipher, or into universality," he optimistically stated the possibilities immanent in the white author's situation. The writer of comprehensive soul who dared to project his experiences on a broad plane would stand at the head of a great tradition. According to Emerson, the world surrounding such a person—that supposedly void externality—offered all the necessary supports. The permanence and importance of works such as Edwards's *Personal Narrative*, Whitman's *Leaves of Grass*, and Adams's *The Education of Henry Adams* in American literature confirm his insight. As the American autobiographer turned inward to seek "the deepest *whole* self of man" (Lawrence's phrase), he carried with him the preexistent codes of his culture. They aided his definition of self and are fully reflected in the resultant texts—self-conscious literary autobiographies.

This perspective on white American autobiography highlights the distinctions between two cultures. Moved to introspection by the apparent "blankness" that surrounded him, the black, southern field slave had scarcely any a priori assumptions to act as stays in his quest for self-definition. He was a man of the diaspora, a displaced person imprisoned by an inhumane system. He was among alien gods in a strange land. Vassa describes his initial placement in the New World:

> We were landed up a river a good way from the sea, *about Virginia country*, where we saw few or none of our native Africans, and not one soul who could talk to me. I was a few weeks weeding grass and gathering stones in a plantation; and at last all my companions were distributed different ways, and only myself was left. I was now exceedingly miserable, and thought myself worse off than any of the rest of my companions, for they could talk to each other, but I had no person to speak to that I could understand. In this state, I was constantly grieving and pining, and wishing for death rather than anything else. [*Life*, p. 34]

For the black slave, the white externality provided no ontological or ideological certainties; in fact, it explicitly denied slaves the grounds of being. The seventeenth- and eighteenth-century black codes defined blacks as slaves in perpetuity, removing their chance to become free, participating citizens in the American city of God. The Constitution reaffirmed the slave's bondage, and the repressive legislation of the nineteenth century categorized him as "chattel personal." Instead of the ebullient sense of a new land offering limitless opportunities, the slave, staring into the heart of whiteness around him, must have felt as though he had been flung into existence without a human purpose. The white externality must have loomed like the Heideggerian "nothingness," the negative foundation of being. Jean Wahl's characterization of Heidegger's theory of existence captures the point of view a black American slave might justifiably have held: "Man is in this world, a world limited by death and experienced in anguish; is aware of himself as essentially anxious; is burdened by his solitude within the horizon of his temporality."[5]

There were at least two alternatives to this vision. There was the recourse of gazing idealistically back to "Guinea." Sterling Stuckey has shown that a small, but vocal, minority of blacks have always employed this strategy.[6] And we have already considered its employment in the work of a northern spokeswoman like Wheatley or a black abolitionist like Vassa. There was also the possibility of adopting the God of the enslaver as solace. A larger number of blacks chose this option and looked to the apocalyptic day that would bring their release from captivity and vengeance on the oppressors. (Tony McNeill's words, "between Africa and heaven," come to mind.) Finally, though, the picture that emerges from the innumerable accounts of slaves is charged with anguish—an anguish that reveals the black bondsman to himself as cast into the world, forlorn and without refuge.

And unlike white Americans who could assume literacy and familiarity with existing literary models as norms, the slave found himself without a system of written language—"uneducated," in the denotative sense of the word. His task was not simply one of moving toward the requisite largeness of soul and faith in the value of his experiences. He first had to seize the word. His being had to erupt from nothingness. Only by grasping the word could he engage in the speech acts that would ultimately define his selfhood. Further, the slave's task was primarily one of creating a human and liberated self rather than of projecting one that reflected a peculiar landscape and tradition. His problem was not to answer Crèvecoeur's question: "What then is the American, this new man?" It was, rather, the problem of being itself.

The *Narrative of the Life of Frederick Douglass,* one of the finest black American slave narratives, serves to illustrate the black autobiographer's quest for being.[7] The recovered past, the journey back, represented in the work is a sparse existence characterized by brutality and uncertainty:

> I have no accurate knowledge of my age. The opinion was . . . whispered about that my master was my father; but of the correctness of this opinion, I know nothing. [Pp. 21–22]

> My mother and I were separated when I was but an infant. [P. 22]

> I was seldom whipped by my old master, and suffered little from anything else than hunger and cold. [P. 43]

> Our food was coarse corn meal boiled. This was called *mush.* It was put into a large wooden trough, and set down upon the ground. The children were then called, like so many pigs, and like so many pigs they would come out and devour the mush. [P. 44]

Unlike David Walker who, in his *Appeal,* attempts to explain why blacks are violently held in bondage, the young Douglass finds no explanation for his condition. And though he does describe the treatment of fellow slaves (including members of his own family), the impression left by the first half of the *Narrative* is one of a lone existence plagued by anxiety. The white world rigorously suppresses all knowledge and action that might lead the narrator to a sense of his humanity.

The total process through which this subjugation is achieved can be seen as an instance of the imposed silence suggested by Forten's address. Mr. Hugh Auld, whom Douglass is sent to serve in Baltimore, finding that his wife—out of an impulse to kindness rare among whites in the *Narrative*—has begun to instruct the slave in the fundamentals of language, vociferously objects that "learning would *spoil* the best nigger in the world." Not only is it illegal to teach slaves, but it is also folly. It makes them aspire to exalted positions. The narrator's reaction to this injunction might be equated with the "dizziness" that, according to Heidegger, accompanies a sudden awareness of possibilities that lie beyond anguish:

> These words sank into my heart, stirred up sentiments within that lay slumbering, and called into existence an entirely new train of thought. It was a new and special revelation, explaining dark and mysterious things, with which my youthful understanding had struggled, but struggled in vain. I now understood what had been to me a most perplexing difficulty—to wit, the white man's power to enslave the black man. [*Narrative*, p. 49]

Douglass had come to understand, by the "merest accident," the power of the word. His future is determined by this moment of revelation: he resolves, "at whatever cost of trouble, to learn how to read." He begins to detach himself from the white externality around him, declaring:

> What he [Mr. Auld] most dreaded, that I most desired. What he most loved, that I most hated. That which to him was a great evil, to be carefully shunned, was to me a great good to be diligently sought; and the argument which he so warmly urged, against my learning to read, only served to inspire me with a desire and determination to learn. [*Narrative*, p. 50]

The balanced antithesis of the passage is but another example—an explicit and forceful one—of the semantic competition involved in culture contact. Mr. Auld is a representation of those whites who felt that by superimposing the cultural sign *nigger* on vibrant human beings like Douglass, they would be able to control the meanings and possibilities of life in America. One marker for the term *nigger* in Auld's semantic field is ⟨⟨subhuman agency of labor⟩⟩. What terrifies and angers the master, however, is that Douglass's capacities—as revealed by his response to Mrs. Auld's kindness and instructions—are not accurately defined by this marker. For Douglass and others of his group are capable of learning. Hence, the markers in Auld's mapping of *nigger* must also include ⟨⟨agent capable of education⟩⟩. The semantic complexity, indeed the wrenching irony, of Auld's "nigger" is forcefully illustrated by the fact that the representation of Auld and *his* point of view enters the world of the learned by way of a narrative written by a "nigger." Douglass, that is to say, ultimately controls the competition among the various markers of *nigger* because he has employed meanings (e.g., agent having the power of literacy) drawn from his own field of experience to represent the competition in a way that invalidates ⟨⟨subhuman agency of labor⟩⟩. The nature of the autobiographical act, in this instance, is one of self-enfolding ironies. Douglass, the literate narrator, represents a Douglass who is perceived by Auld as a "nigger." Certainly the narrator himself, who is a learned writer, can see this "nigger" only through Auld, who is the "other." And it is the "otherness" of Auld that is both repudiated and controlled by the narrator's balanced antithesis. By converting the otherness of Auld (and, consequently, his "nigger") into discourse, Douglass becomes the master of his own situation. And the white man, who wants a silently laboring brute, is finally (and ironically) visible to himself and a learned reading public only through the discourse of the articulate black spokesman.

Much of the remainder of the *Narrative* counterpoints the assumption of the white world that the slave is a brute[8] against the slave's expanding awareness of language and its capacity to carry him toward new dimensions of experience. Chapter seven (the one following the Auld encounter), for example, is devoted to Douglass's increasing command of the word. He discovers *The Columbian Orator*, with its striking messages of human dignity and freedom and its practical examples of the results of fine speaking. He also learns the significance of that all-important word *abolition*. Against these new perceptions, he juxtaposes the unthinking condition of slaves who have not yet acquired language skills equal to his own. At times he envies them, since they (like the "meanest reptile") are not fully and self-consciously aware of their situation. For the narrator, language brings the possibility of freedom but renders slavery intolerable. It gives rise to his decision to escape as soon as his age and the opportunity are appropriate. Meanwhile, he bides his time and perfects his writing, since (as he says in a telling act of autobiographical conflation) "I might have occasion to write my own pass" (*Narrative*, p. 57).

Douglass's description of his reaction to ships on the Chesapeake illustrates that he did, effectively, write his own pass: "Those beautiful vessels, robed in purest white, so delightful to the eye of freemen, were to me so many shrouded ghosts to terrify and torment me with thoughts of my wretched condition" (*Narrative*, p. 76). He continues with a passionate apostrophe that shows how dichotomous are his own condition and that of these white, "swift-winged angels."

> You are loosed from your moorings, and are free: I am fast in my chains, and am a slave! You move merrily before the gentle gale, and I sadly before the bloody whip! You are freedom's swift-winged angels, that fly around the world; I am confined in bands of iron! O that I were free! O, that I were on one of your gallant decks, and under your protecting wing! Alas! betwixt me and you, the turbid waters roll. Go on, go on. O that I could also go! Could I but swim! If I could fly! O, why was I born a man, of whom to make a brute! The glad ship is gone; she hides in the dim distance. I am left in the hottest hell of unending slavery. O God, save me! God, deliver me! Let me be free! Is there any God? Why am I a slave? I will run away. I will not stand it. Get caught, or get clear, I'll try it. [*Narrative*, p. 76]

When clarified and understood through language, the deathly, terrifying nothingness around him reveals the grounds of being. Freedom, the ability to chose one's own direction, makes life beautiful and pure. Only the man free from bondage has a chance to obtain the farthest reaches of humanity. From what appears a blank and awesome backdrop, Douglass wrests significance. His subsequent progression through the roles of educated leader, freeman, abolitionist, and autobiographer marks his firm sense of being.

But while it is the fact that the ships are loosed from their moorings that intrigues the narrator, he also drives home their whiteness and places them in a Christian context. Here certain added difficulties for the black autobiographer reveal themselves. The acquisition of language, which leads to being, has ramifications that have been best stated by the West Indian novelist George Lamming, drawing on the relationship between Prospero and Caliban in *The Tempest:*

> Prospero has given Caliban Language; and with it an unstated history of consequences, an unknown history of future intentions. This gift of language meant not English, in particular, but speech and concept as a way, a method, a necessary avenue towards areas of the self which could not be reached in any other way. It is in this way, entirely Prospero's enterprise, which makes Caliban aware of possibilities. Therefore, all of Caliban's future—for future is the very name for possibilities—must derive from Prospero's experiment, which is also his risk.[9]

Mr. Auld had seen that "learning" could lead to the restiveness of his slave. Neither he nor his representer, however, seem to understand that it might be possible to imprison the slave even more thoroughly in the way described by Lamming. The angelic Mrs. Auld, however, in accord with the evangelical codes of her era, has given Douglass the rudiments of a system that leads to intriguing restrictions. True, the slave can arrive at a sense of being only through language. But it is also true that, in Douglass's case, a conception of the preeminent form of being is conditioned by white, Christian standards.

To say this is not to charge him with treachery. Africa was for the black southern slave an idealized backdrop, which failed to offer the immediate tangible means of his liberation. Moreover, whites continually sought to strip Africans of their distinctive cultural modes. Vassa's isolation and perplexity upon his arrival in the New World, which are recorded in a passage previously cited, give some notion of the results of this white offensive. Unable to transplant the institutions of his homeland in the soil of America—as the Puritans had done—the black slave had to seek means of survival and fulfillment on that middle ground where the European slave trade had deposited him. He had to seize whatever weapons came to hand in his struggle for self-definition. The range of instruments was limited. Evangelical Christians and committed abolitionists were the only discernible groups standing in the path of America's hypocrisy and inhumanity. The dictates of these groups, therefore, suggested a way beyond servitude. And these were the only signs and wonders in an environment where blacks were deemed animals, or "things." Determined to move beyond a subservient status, cut off from the alternatives held out to whites, endowed with the "feeling" that freedom is the natural condition of life, Douglass adopted a system of symbols that seemed to promise him an unbounded freedom. Having acquired language and a set of dictates that specified freedom and equality as norms, Douglass becomes more assured. His certainty is reflected by the roles he projects for himself in the latter part of his *Narrative*. They are all in harmony with a white, Christian, abolitionist framework.

During his year at Mr. Freeland's farm, for example, he spends much of his time "doing something that looked like bettering the condition of my race" (*Narrative*, p. 90). His enterprise is a Sabbath school devoted to teaching his "loved fellow-slaves" so they will be able "to read the will of God" (*Narrative*, p. 89). His efforts combine the philanthropic impulse of the eighteenth-century man of sympathy with a zeal akin to Jupiter Hammon's.

Having returned to Mr. Auld's house after an absence of three years, he undertakes a useful trade and earns the right to hire out his own time. All goes well until he attends a religious camp meeting one Saturday night and fails to pay the allotted weekly portion of his wages to his master. When Auld rebukes him, the demands of the "robber" are set against the natural right of a man to worship God freely. Once again, freedom is placed in a Christian context. Infuriated, Douglass decides that the time and circumstances are now right for his escape. When he arrives in New York, he feels like a man who has "escaped a den of hungry lions" (a kind of New World Daniel), and one of his first acts is to marry Anna Murray in a Christian ceremony presided over by the Reverend James W. C. Pennington. It would not be an overstatement to say that the liberated self portrayed by Douglass is firmly Christian, having adopted cherished values from the white world that held him in bondage. It is not surprising, therefore, to see the narrator moving rapidly into the ranks of the abolitionists—that body of men and women bent on putting America in harmony with its professed ideals. Nor is it striking that the *Narrative* concludes with an appendix in which the narrator justifies himself as a true Christian.

In recovering the details of his past, then, the autobiographer shows a progression from baffled and isolated existent to Christian abolitionist lecturer and writer. The self in the autobiographical moment (the present, the time in which the work is composed), however, seems unaware of the limitations that have accompanied this progress. Even though the writer seems to have been certain (given the cohesiveness of the *Narrative*) how he was going to picture his development and how the emergent self should appear to the reader, he seems to have suppressed the fact that one cannot transcend existence in a universe where there is *only* existence. One can realize one's humanity through "speech and concept," but one cannot distinguish the uniqueness of the self if the "avenue towards areas of the self" excludes rigorously individualizing definitions of a human, black identity.

Douglass grasps language in a Promethean act of will, but he leaves unexamined its potentially devastating effects. One reflection of his uncritical acceptance of the perspective made available by literacy is the *Narrative* itself, which was written at the urging of white abolitionists who had become the fugitive slave's employers. The work was written to prove that the narrator had indeed been a slave. And while autobiographical conventions forced him to portray as accurately as possible the existentiality of his original condition, the light of abolitionism is always implicitly present, guiding the narrator into calm, Christian, and publicly accessible harbors. The issue here is not simply one of intentionality (how the author wished his utterances to be taken). It is, rather, one that combines Douglass's understandable desire to keep his job with more complex considerations governing "privacy" as a philosophical concept.

Language, like other social institutions, is public; it is one of the surest means we have of communicating with the "other," the world outside ourselves. Moreover, since language seems to provide the principal way in which we conceptualize and convey anything (thoughts, feelings, sensations, and so forth), it is possible that no easily describable "private" domain exists. By adopting language as his instrument for extracting meaning from nothingness, being from existence, Douglass becomes a public figure.

He is comforted, but also restricted, by the system he adopts. The results are shown in the hierarchy of preferences that, finally, constitute value in the *Narrative*. The results are additionally demonstrated by those instances in the *Narrative* where the work's style is indistinguishable from that of the sentimental-romantic oratory and creative writing that marked the American nineteenth century. Had there been a separate, written black language available, Douglass might have fared better. What is seminal to this discussion, however, is that the nature of the autobiographer's situation seemed to force him to move to a public version of the self—one molded by the values of white America. Thus Mr. Auld can be contained and controlled within the slave narrator's abolitionist discourse because Auld is a stock figure of such discourse. He is the penurious master corrupted by the soul-killing effects of slavery who appears in poetry, fiction, and polemics devoted to the abolitionist cause.

But the slave narrator must also accomplish the almost unthinkable (since thought and language are inseparable) task of transmuting an authentic, unwritten self—a self that exists outside the conventional literary discourse structures of a white reading public—into a literary representation. The simplest, and perhaps the most effective, way of proceeding is for the narrator to represent his "authentic" self as a figure embodying the public virtues and values esteemed by his intended audience. Once he has seized the public medium, the slave narrator can construct a public message, or massage, calculated to win approval for himself and (provided he has one) his cause. In the white abolitionist William

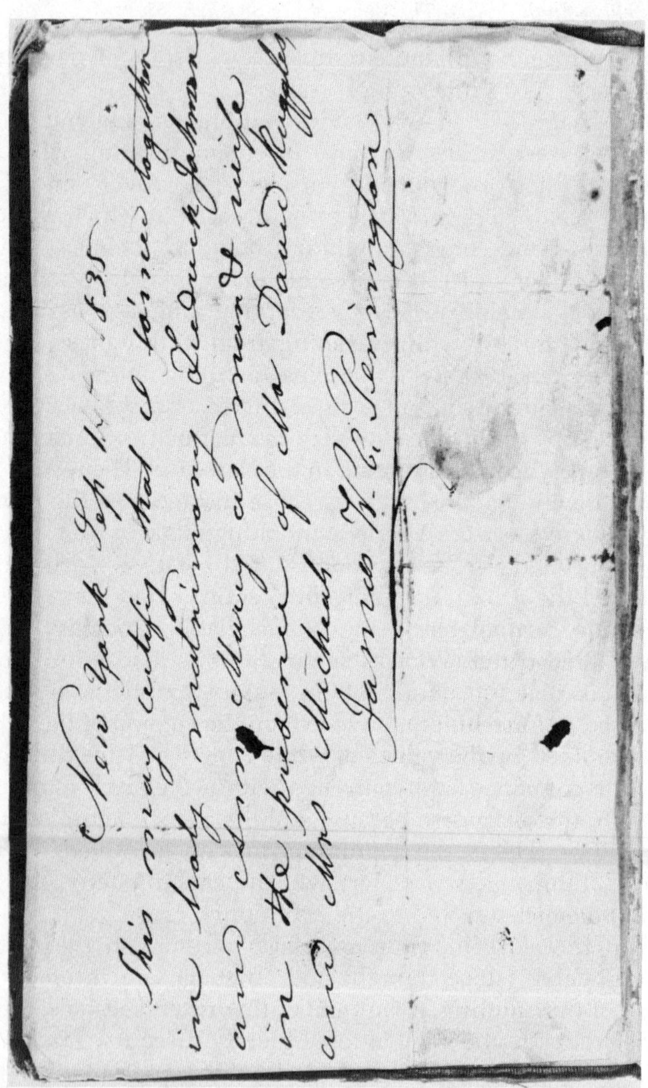

New York Sep 15 1838

This may certify that I joined together
in holy matrimony Frederick Johnson
and Anna Murray as man & wife
in the presence of Mr David Ruggles
and Mrs Michaels

James W. C. Pennington

Title page of a copy of the 1849 edition of Frederick Douglass's *Narrative* . Pasted on the flyleaf is the certificate of marriage given to Douglass and Anna Murray by the Reverend James W. C. Pennington. Douglass, who began life with the name Bailey, changed his name to Johnson on escaping bondage

NARRATIVE

OF THE

LIFE

OF

FREDERICK DOUGLASS,

AN

AMERICAN SLAVE.

WRITTEN BY HIMSELF.

BOSTON:

PUBLISHED AT THE ANTI-SLAVERY OFFICE,

No. 25 CORNHILL.

1849

and then to Douglass on arriving in New Bedford, Massachusetts, because "there were so many Johnsons in New Bedford, it was already quite difficult to distinguish between them." (Photographs from the Moorland-Spingarn Research Center, Frederick Douglass Collection.)

Lloyd Garrison's preface to Douglass's *Narrative,* for example, the slave narrator is elaborately praised for his seemingly godlike movement "into the field of public usefulness" (*Narrative,* pp.v–vi). Garrison writes of his own reaction to Douglass's first abolitionist lecture to a white audience:

> I shall never forget his first speech at the convention—the extraordinary emotion it excited in my own mind—the powerful impression it created upon a crowded auditory, completely taken by surpise—the applause which followed from the beginning to the end of his felicitous remarks. I think I never hated slavery so intensely as at that moment; certainly, my perception of the enormous outrage which is inflicted by it, on the godlike nature of its victims, was rendered far more clear than ever. There stood one, in physical proportion and stature commanding and exact—in intellect richly endowed—in natural eloquence a prodigy—in soul manifestly "created but a little lower than the angels"—trembling for his safety, hardly daring to believe that on the American soil, a single white person could be found who would befriend him at all hazards, for the love of God and humanity. Capable of high attainments as an intellectual and moral being—needing nothing but a comparatively small amount of cultivation to make him an ornament to society and a blessing to his race—by the law of the land, by the voice of the people, by the terms of the slave code, he was only a piece of property, a beast of burden, a chattel personal, nevertheless! [*Narrative,* p. vi]

Obviously, a talented, heroic, and richly endowed figure such as Garrison describes here was of inestimable "public usefulness" to the abolitionist crusade. And the Nantucket Convention of 1841 where Garrison first heard Douglass speak may be compared to a communicative context in which the sender and receiver employ a common channel (i.e., the English language) to arrive at, or to reinforce for each other, an agreed-upon message. Douglass transmits the "heroic fugitive" message to an abolitionist audience that has made such a figure part of its conceptual, linguistic, and rhetorical repertoire.

The issue that such an "autobiographical" act raises for the literary analyst is that of authenticity. Where, for example, in Douglass's *Narrative* does a prototypical black American self reside? What are the distinctive narrative elements that combine to form a representation of this self? In light of the foregoing discussion, it seems that such elements would be located in those episodes and passages of the *Narrative* that chronicle the struggle for literacy. For once literacy has been achieved, the black self, even as represented in the *Narrative*, begins to distance itself from the domain of experience constituted by the oral-aural community of the slave quarters (e.g., the remarks comparing fellow slaves to the meanest reptiles). The voice of the unwritten self, once it is subjected to the linguistic codes, literary conventions, and audience expectations of a literate population, is perhaps never again the authentic voice of black American slavery. It is, rather, the voice of a self transformed by an autobiographical act into a sharer in the general public discourse about slavery.

How much of the lived (as opposed to the represented) slave experience is lost in this transformation depends upon the keenness of the narrator's skill in confronting both the freedom and the limitations resulting from his literacy in Prospero's tongue. By the conclusion of Douglass's *Narrative*, the represented self seems to have left the quarters almost entirely behind. The self that appears in the work's closing moments is that of a public spokesman, talking about slavery to a Nantucket convention of whites:

> while attending an anti-slavery convention at Nantucket, on the 11th of August, 1841, I felt strongly moved to speak, and was at the same time much urged to do so by Mr. William C. Coffin, a gentleman who had heard me speak in the colored people's meeting at New Bedford. It was a severe cross, and I took it up reluctantly. The truth was, I felt myself a slave, and the idea of speaking to white people weighed me down. I spoke but a few moments, when I felt a degree of freedom, and said what I desired with considerable ease. From that time until now, I have been engaged in pleading the cause of my brethren—with what success, and with what devotion, I leave to those acquainted with my labors to decide. [*Narrative*, pp. 118–19]

The Christian imagery ("a severe cross"), strained reluctance to speak before whites, discovered ease of eloquence, and public-spirited devotion to the cause of his brethren that appear in this passage are all in keeping with the image of the publicly useful and ideal fugitive captured in Garrison's preface. Immediately before telling the reader of his address to the Nantucket convention, Douglass notes that "he had not long been a reader of the 'Liberator' [Garrison's abolitionist newspaper]" before he got "a pretty correct idea of the principles, measures and spirit of the anti-slavery reform"; he adds that he "took right hold of the cause . . . and never felt happier than when in an anti-slavery meeting" (*Narrative*, p. 118). This suggests to me that the communication between Douglass and Garrison begins long before their face-to-face encounter at Nantucket, with the fugitive slave's culling from the white publisher's newspaper those virtues and values esteemed by abolitionist readers. The fugitive's voice is further refined by his attendance and speeches at the "colored people's meeting at New Bedford," and it finally achieves its emotionally stirring participation in the white world of public discourse at the 1841 Nantucket convention.

Of course, there are tangible reasons within the historical (as opposed to the autobiographical) domain for the image that Douglass projects. The feeling of larger goals shared with a white majority culture has always been present among blacks. We need only turn back to the earlier discussion of Hammon, Wheatley, and Vassa to see this. From at least the third decade of the nineteenth century this feeling of a common pursuit was reinforced by men like Garrison and Wendall Phillips, by constitutional amendments, civil rights legislation, and perennial assurances that the white man's dream is the black man's as well. Furthermore, what better support for this assumption of commonality could Douglass find than in his own palpable achievements in American society?

When he revised his original *Narrative* for the third time, therefore, in 1893, the work that resulted represented the conclusion of a process that began for Douglass at the home of Hugh Auld. *The Life and Times of Frederick Douglass Written by Himself* is public, rooted in the language of its time, and considerably less existential in tone than the 1845 *Narrative*. What we have is a verbose and somewhat hackneyed story of a life, written by a man of achievement. The white externality has been transformed into a world where sterling deeds by blacks are possible. Douglass describes his visit to the home of his former master who, forty years after the slave's escape, now rests on his deathbed:

> On reaching the house I was met by Mr. Wm. H. Buff, a son-in-law of Capt. Auld, and Mrs. Louisa Buff, his daughter, and was conducted to the bedroom of Capt. Auld. We addressed each other simultaneously, he called me "Marshal Douglass," and I, as I had always called him, "Captain Auld." Hearing myself called by him "Marshal Douglass," I instantly broke up the formal nature of the meeting by saying, "not *Marshal*, but Frederick to you as formerly." We shook hands cordially and in the act of doing so, he, having been long stricken with palsy, shed tears as men thus afflicted will do when excited by any deep emotion. The sight of him, the changes which time had wrought in him, his tremulous hands constantly in motion, and all the circumstances of his condition affected me deeply, and for a time choked my voice and made me speechless.[10]

A nearly tearful silence by the black "Marshal" (a term repeated three times in very brief space) of the District of Columbia as he gazes with sympathy on the body of his former master—this is a great distance, to be sure, from the aggressive young slave who appropriated language in order to do battle with the masters.

A further instance of Douglass's revised perspective is provided by his return to the home plantation of Colonel Lloyd on the Wye River in Talbot County, Maryland:

> Speaking of this desire of mine [to revisit the Lloyd Plantation] last winter, to Hon. John L. Thomas, the efficient collector at the Port of Baltimore, and a leading Republican of the State of Maryland, he urged me very much to go, and added that he often took a trip to the Eastern Shore in his revenue cutter *Guthrie* (otherwise known in time of war as the *Ewing*), and would be much pleased to have me accompany him on

> one of these trips. . . . In four hours after leaving Baltimore we were anchored in the river off the Lloyd estate, and from the deck of our vessel I saw once more the stately chimneys of the grand old mansion which I had last seen from the deck of the *Sally Lloyd* when a boy. I left there as a slave, and returned as a freeman; I left there unknown to the outside world, and returned well known; I left there on a freight boat and returned on a revenue cutter; I left on a vessel belonging to Col. Edward Lloyd, and returned on one belonging to the United States. [*Life and Times,* pp. 445–46]

The "stately chimneys of the grand old mansion" sounds very much like the Plantation Tradition, and how different the purpose of the balanced antithesis is in this passage from that noted in the delineation of the slave's realization of language as a key to freedom ("What he most dreaded, that I most desired . . ."). This passage also stands in marked contrast to the description of ships on the Chesapeake cited earlier ("those beautiful vessels . . . so many shrouded ghosts"). The venerable status of the *Guthrie* is now matched by the eminence of the marshal of the District of Columbia.

Douglass, in his public role, often resembles the courteous and gentlemanly narrator of Vassa's work—a man determined to put readers at ease by assuring them of his accomplishments (and the sterling company he keeps) in language that is careful not to offend readers' various sensibilities. It is strikingly coincidental that *The Life and Times of Frederick Douglass* was reprinted in 1895, the year in which its author died and Booker T. Washington emerged as one of the most influential black public spokesmen America had ever known.

In 1901, Washington's *Up from Slavery* appeared, and it offers a perfect illustration of the black autobiographer's assumption of the public mantle. Unlike Douglass's 1845 *Narrative* (but like the 1893 version), Washington's work is primarily a life-and-times account that views the self within the larger American social current. Instead of apology, or the justification of rebellion, one finds in *Up from Slavery* gratitude—even joy—that the self has been swept along by the current and acknowledged for aiding its progressive flow. Moral uplift and financial success quickly run together as Washington accepts Economic Man as the norm in his own ascent from ignorance, poverty, and vice to property-ownership and a sound bank account. Of course, the first president of Tuskegee Institute cannot be immediately denounced for portraying himself in this manner, since such a condemnation would require censuring the entire age in which he lived. Situated in the Gilded Age and surrounded by a set of conditions that the historian Rayford Logan has called the "nadir" in American race relations, Washington adopted a public mask that displayed a black self in harmony with its era. The problem with this strategy was that it forced the narrator to violate the governing conventions of autobiography at the very outset. He set truth aside from the beginning and simply ignored facts that did not agree with his mask.

Washington, therefore, is no bold historian who has surveyed chaos and given us the verifiable details of his journey. We cannot grasp the uniqueness of a black self because a self distinguishable from those of Huntington, Carnegie, Vanderbilt, and other white capitalists never emerges. Further, the sense that black being can emerge only by erupting through a white nothingness is contradicted by the countless white friends who aid Washington on his way to language, education, and financial stability. Rebecca Chalmers Barton has defined Washington and all black autobiographers who followed his lead as "accommodators," i.e., pseudoidealists who concealed their ambitiousness and feelings of inferiority in religious rhetoric and oratory dedicated to a cause.[11] Given the nature of *Up from Slavery*, this assessment seems just. It is difficult to understand how a more recent writer[12] has set such store by those turn-of-the-century black autobiographies which, time and again, reveal their narrators drawn into the linguistic prisons—the confining public discourse—of the white world.

Difficult, but not impossible. For if one takes language in a broad social sense and treats *Up from Slavery* as a social document, then Washington was simply an imitator of the commerical, industrial utterances that guided his age. His narrative is filled with the kind of observation one would expect to find in a primer devoted to principles of success in business and the conduct of the moral life in an industrialist society:

> One thing I was determined to do from the first, and that was to keep the credit of the school high, and this, I think I can say without boasting, we have done all through these years. I shall always remember a bit of advice given me by Mr. George W. Campbell, the white man to whom I have referred as the one who induced General Armstrong to send me to Tuskegee. Soon after I entered upon the work Mr. Campbell said to me, in his fatherly way: "Washington, always remember that credit is capital."[13]

On the subject of soliciting contributions for Tuskegee:

> Such work gives one a rare opportunity to study human nature. It also has its compensation in giving one an opportunity to meet some of the best people in the world—to be more correct, I think I should say *the best* people in the world. When one takes a broad survey of the country, he will find that the most useful and influential people in it are those who take the deepest interest in institutions that exist for the purpose of making the world better. [P. 127]

On interaction with the wealthy:

> I have found that strict business methods go a long way in securing the interest of rich people. It has been my constant aim at Tuskegee to carry out, in our financial and other operations, such business methods as would be approved of by any New York banking house. [P. 132]

Two of his improving maxims read:

> In meeting men, in many places, I have found that the happiest people are those who do the most for others; the most miserable are those who do the least. I have also found that few things, if any, are capable of making one so blind and narrow as race prejudice. [P. 152]

> I have a strong feeling that every individual owes it to himself, and to the cause which he is serving, to keep a vigorous, healthy body, with the nerves steady and strong, prepared for

> great efforts and prepared for disappointments and trying positions. [P. 171]

Finally, one of the most infamous examples of Washington's employment of the language and concepts of the commercial industrial estate of his era appears in his speech to the Atlanta Cotton States and International Exposition, which was delivered in 1895, and which is set down in full in *Up from Slavery*. He advises his recently emancipated fellow blacks:

> when it comes to business, pure and simple, it is in the South that the Negro is given a man's chance in the commercial world, and in nothing is this Exposition more eloquent than in emphasizing this chance. Our greatest danger is that in the great leap from slavery to freedom we may overlook the fact that the masses of us are to live by the productions of our hands, and fail to keep in mind that we shall prosper in proportion as we learn to dignify and glorify common labour and put brains and skill into the common occupations of life . . . . It is at the bottom of life we must begin, and not at the top. [*Up from Slavery*, p. 147]

Founded on the assumption that only through hard work and abundant evidence that one has something to contribute to the white community can the black American rise, Washington's statement implicitly sanctioned the violently racist practices of his day. When Governor Bullock of Georgia introduced him at the Exposition as "a representative of Negro enterprise and Negro civilization," he surely had a clear idea of the type of representation of black life and culture Washington would present. The occasion, as it appears in *Up from Slavery*, is yet another instance of the coming together of a white audience and a black speaker who has molded a publicly useful "autobiographical" self. In Washington's case, unfortunately, Governor Bullock (and not William Lloyd Garrison) was the exemplary member of the white audience. Thus Washington, as a black public spokesman, became the compromiser of his own people's rights, and the Barton view of the author of *Up from Slavery* is reinforced by an analysis of the work as a social document.

But if language is considered not in the broad social sense but in the more restricted context of fictive discourse, then Washington's narrative, as a fictive account, presents a coherent structure signaling a particular domain of meaning. Rather than the "pseudoidealism" deplored by Barton, it implies propositions of the form "If X then Y."[14] For example, the world of the slave is one of unlimited opportunity; the black man can, if only he will. This amounts to a tacit agreement between the propositions governing *Up from Slavery* and the professed ideals of the larger white American culture. The work is designed as a validation of what the psychologists Hans Vaihinger and Alfred Adler called "fictional ideas" or "fictional finalism."[15] The notion captured by these phrases is that human beings are motivated in their present actions by their expectations of the future, by their orientation toward a goal which has no counterpart in reality. "This final goal may be a fiction, that is, an ideal that is impossible to realize but which is nonetheless a very real spur to human striving and the ultimate explanation of conduct."[16] Statements such as "all men are created equal," that is to say, or "honesty is the best policy," govern conduct. Washington's work, under the aspect of fictive discourse, can be interpreted as saying: "The propositions are analytic (basic, beyond question). Here is a story to prove it." In this light, *Up from Slavery* offers a stirring account. The differences between black and white fade; the disruptions of the triangular trade and chattel slavery are excusable failings of a past that is best forgotten. The motivation is directed entirely toward the future.

The problem with this interpretive strategy, however, is that while it provides one means of apprehending and valuing the text, it also ignores the significant conventions surrounding the genre that Washington and his cohorts chose to employ. Autobiography—the recounting of the self's or the selves' history—does not presuppose analytic propositions. It is, rather, a gathering together of synthetic propositions—factual statements whose truth-value is assumed to be historically determinate. Its statements are taken to accord with an actual past that is amenable to investigation. The difference between the fictive and the autobiographical can be suggested by the responses each entails to a statement like the following:

> The "Ku Klux" period was, I think, the darkest part of the Reconstruction days. I have referred to this unpleasant part of the history of the South simply for the purpose of calling attention to the great change that has taken place since the days of the "Ku Klux." To-day there are no such organizations in the South, and the fact that such ever existed is almost forgotten by both races. There are few places in the South now where public sentiment would permit such organizations to exist. [*Up from Slavery*, p. 71]

The truth-value of this assertion if it appeared in a novel would not be a very fruitful analytical issue to pursue. In an autobiography, however, the statement must be set against historical evidence as we know it. Only then can a reader judge the author's relationship to fundamental conventions, or rules, of the autobiographical genre.[17] And in the example cited, the narrator's assertion is a patent falsification.

One cannot dismiss Washington's work, however, as simply the effort of a writer confused about two realms of discourse, the fictive and the autobiographical. There is no more justification for such a course than there is for ignoring Wheatley because she used heroic couplets. What is demanded from the literary investigator is an analysis that will reveal the intersections between the two worlds of discourse. This discovery might lead, in turn, to a wider inquiry into the nature of black narrative. The school of "accommodators" can serve as a starting point, that is to say, in the search for higher-order rules that condition the fictionalizing of the self in autobiography and the construction of an autobiographical self in fiction that mark such narratives as Richard Wright's *Black Boy* and James Weldon Johnson's *The Autobiography of an Ex-Colored Man.* The question is how such works achieve their effects and eventually come to hold valued positions in black intellectual and literary history.

Though Washington's voice is surely not the one Forten had in mind when he spoke of the slaves who might trouble their masters' quiet, it is nonetheless a distinctive voice and raises its own set of problems about Caliban's presence in the New World. *Up From Slavery*, like Wheatley's poetry and Vassa's narrative, stands as a verbal structure that compels our attention. If it falsifies details of the journey, it promises much for our understanding of the voyage into language. The wholeness of the self, the self as public man, the autobiographical self engaged in fictive discourse—these, too, represent attempts to find terms for order in a complex world.

The culturally unique aspects of *Up from Slavery* reside, like those in the works of the authors already discussed, at a level of functional oppositions. In this case, the disparity is between a graphically depicted hell of rural, impoverished, illiterate black southern life and an intriguingly displayed heaven of black southern urbanity, thrift, and education. Two distinct modes of discourse sustain this opposition—the autobiographical self exists in the former, while the fictive self lives in (and testifies to the possibility of) the latter.

3 *Sightings: Black Historical Consciousness and the New Harbors of the Fifties*

By the time Washington's work appeared, black writers had already begun to map the ground in different ways. The southern utopia was never to become a reality. Already, blacks were moving northward. More than two million departed between 1890 and 1920. Terms for order would have to become more exacting as a free black multitude made its way into the urban, industrial world. It is here that the field becomes dense. The proliferation of voices rises to a crescendo in the Harlem Renaissance of the 1920s. The world of twentieth-century black writing has witnessed the chronicling of the journey by Jean Toomer, Langston Hughes, Zora Neale Hurston, Richard Wright, and so many others who are notable. It is only in recent years, however, that black writers as an extensive and articulate group have been able to travel all the way back to origins and record their insights in distinctive forms designed for a black audience. Some steps which were necessary before this could occur have already been traced. The resistance to white hegemony, the preservation of unique meanings in the black semantic domain, the seizure of language as a weapon of liberation and being, the employment of distinctive literary strategies that led to unique verbal structures—all of these have resulted in works of art that allow one to chart the way back. It

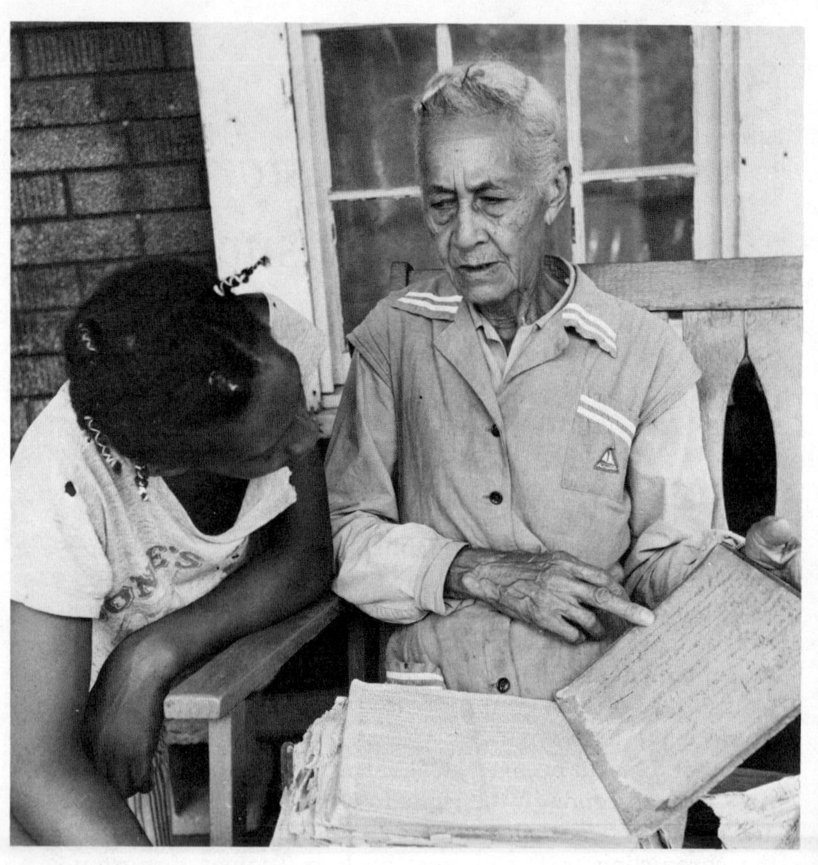

was in essence the socially and politically motivated encounters with the facts governing these steps that engaged the black writer's attention in the years between 1954 and 1976.

During this period, black writers moved to a linguistic sophistication and a historical clarity that seemed to augur, if not to create, the very imperium in imperio that had existed previously only as an idea in the black American consciousness. The black past did not become less difficult to navigate during these years, but its black journeymen had become more than equal to the voyage. They saw (as we must all come to perceive) whole worlds of meaning and possibility in the objects, events, and verbal structures that suddenly entered their perceptual field. Witness Ellison's protagonist in *Invisible Man*. Attracted by a dark, sullen crowd and the pleadings of a feeble black woman to "look what they doing to us," he finds himself at the scene of a Harlem eviction. Beside a worn chest that has been placed on the sidewalk, he discovers a fragile paper written in black ink grown yellow:

> FREE PAPERS. *Be it known to all men that my negro, Primus Provo, has been freed by me this sixth day of August, 1859. Signed: John Samuels. Macon* . . . . I folded it quickly, blotting out the single drop of melted snow which glistened on the yellowed page, and dropped it back into the drawer. My hands were trembling, my breath rasping as if I had run a long distance or come upon a coiled snake in a busy street. *It has been longer than that, further, removed in time,* I told myself and yet I knew that it hadn't been.[1]

This is the sudden awakening of a person who has indeed run a long way. A head-on collision with history is revealed in a terse utterance. And the scene's details make it an appropriate emblem for the black writer's response to awesome historical facts that appeared in bold relief during the 1950s.

Turning his gaze inward, the black writer saw what Ellison describes as "all those blasting pressures which in a scant eighty years have sent the Negro people hurtling, without clearly defined trajectory, from slavery to emancipation, from log cabin to city tenement, from the white folks' fields and kitchens to factory assembly lines; and which between two wars, have shattered the wholeness of its folk consciousness into a thousand writhing pieces."[2] If he turned outward and assumed a global frame of reference, he saw the vista described by Richard Wright: "Today, as the tide of white domination of the land mass of Asia and Africa recedes, there lies to view a procession of shattered cultures, disintegrated societies, and a writhing sweep of more aggressive, irrational religion than the world has known for centuries."[3] Both perspectives revealed the coming to full consciousness of the colored peoples of the world. They had been awakened by raucous industrial cities and were abandoning dreams of homogenous rural communities in order to face the overwhelming realities of advanced technological societies. The black writer, like all persons of color, was faced with the question of what to make of a diminished thing and how to fulfill his role in the modern world.

The black American fifties were far from silent. They witnessed the Supreme Court's ruling in *Brown* v. *Board of Education*, which stated that "separate but equal" public school facilities were inherently unequal. They saw the rise to independence of formerly colonized African nations. The Bandung Conference of Asian and African leaders was convened in Indonesia in 1955,[4] and in the same year Mrs. Rosa Parks was arrested for her refusal to give up her seat to a white man and move to the back of a Montgomery bus. The Montgomery bus boycott was thus set in motion, and the Reverend Martin Luther King, Jr., was on his way to becoming one of the most powerful black leaders of this century. Colored people were on the move. They were moving by the hundreds of thousands to large urban areas of the North and West. And they were moving in direct action protests throughout the world. Despite the bombings, murders, and mass arrests, and the halting, stalling resistance on the part of the white world, the prevailing mood of the 1950s was one of optimism. A new moral climate seemed abroad, one conducive to a fully integrated world.[5]

Black writers faced this panorama by asserting their place

on the stage of Western history and by arguing that the old categories and definitions that had left them in the wings were simply distorted products of the European or American imagination. In *Notes of a Native Son* James Baldwin reduces the history of slavery and race relations in America to a Christian psychodrama in which white missionaries associated black Africans with evil and hurried them into the chains of slavery in order to assure the salvation of the white world.[6] In *White Man, Listen!* Richard Wright says:

> Rooted in my own disinheritedness, I know instinctively that this clinging to, and defense of racism by Western whites are born of their psychological nakedness, of their having, through historical accident, partially thrown off the mystic cauls of Asia and Africa that once too blinded and dazed them. A deeply conscious victim of white racism could even be strangely moved to compassion for that white man who, having lost his mystic vision of a stern Father God, a dazzling Virgin, and a Dying Son Who promises to succor him after death, settles upon racism! [P. 49]

And in response to the question, "What do you understand today by 'Negro culture,'" Ralph Ellision wrote:

> What I understand by the term "Negro culture" is so vague as to be meaningless. Indeed, I find the term "Negro" vague even in its racial connotations, for in Africa there are several non-white racial strains and one suspects that the term came into usage as a means of obliterating cultural differences between the various African peoples. In this way the ruthless disruption of highly developed cultures raised no troubling moral questions. The term, used mainly by whites, represented a "trained incapacity" to make or feel moral distinctions where black men were concerned. [*Shadow and Act*, p. 253]

There is a leap of some magnitude between these sharply analytical lines by three of the more prominent recent black writers and Vassa's seemingly awe-struck account of the slave ship. The gaze of the contemporary writers is, however, still turned in the same direction—backward, to a time of chaos. But a significant difference separates Vassa's and the modern writers' perspectives. The world of the latter is much more complex; it does not stretch from a pastoral Africa to a finely cultivated West. Instead, the very nature of the West is at issue for Baldwin, Ellison, and Wright, and Western history reveals itself as a region of contrived corridors and serpentine illusions. Aware of the psychological aberrations fostered in the white West by colonialism and slavery, the black writer faced a suddenly enormous task. His awareness mandated an involved and sophisticated response.

There has always been, as I have emphasized in previous chapters, a strong drive in black culture toward a larger white society. The tacit agreement between Washington's work and the ideals of America, the concurrence between Vassa's "fictional ideas" and those of eighteenth-century England, and the harmony between Douglass's self-representations and the ideals of nineteenth-century Evangelicalism and abolitionism are signs of this impulse. The governing assumption behind such alliances has been that at some deep level, the West unequivocally endorses a set of attitudes and beliefs that motivate social equality. These unimpeachable mental ideals may be veiled for the present, but in time they will surface, giving birth and lending splendor to a new egalitarian world. To speed the birth of this resplendent world, black spokesmen have felt it necessary first to gain language and then to add their voices to a general public discourse on equality. There are also considerations of audience (whom could the literate black author address but a literate Westerner since his own kin remained without the word?) involved here, and they will be taken up later. For the moment, it is sufficient to say that the black writer in the fifties found himself with a far less optimistic view of the possibilities of social equality in the West than the one endorsed by black writers of previous decades. Ironically, though, the alternatives to the paths that his forebears had followed seemed describable only in broadly Western, or American, terms.

Like the civil rights worker in the deep South, the black writer was paradoxically compelled to see himself against a backdrop of ideas and ideals more honored in the breach than in the observance. From the South of the 1950s came black voices raised in the name of the Bill of Rights and the Constitution. And from the lecture platforms of Europe during the same decade came Wright's assertion that "shoulder to shoulder with the Western white man, speaking his tongue, sharing his culture, participating in the common efforts of the Western community, I say frankly to that white man: 'I'm Western, just as Western as you are, maybe more'" (*White Man, Listen!* p. 50). Baldwin wrote of his affiliation in *Notes of a Native Son:*

> I know, in any case, that the most crucial time in my own development came when I was forced to recognize that I was a kind of bastard of the West; when I followed the line of my past I did not find myself in Europe but in Africa. And this meant that in some subtle way, in a really profound way, I brought to Shakespeare, Bach, Rembrandt, to the stones of Paris, the cathedral at Chartres, and to the Empire State Building, a special attitude.... I was an interloper; this was not my heritage. At the same time I had no other heritage which I could possibly hope to use.... I would have to appropriate these white centuries. [Pp. 6–7]

Finally, rounding out a composite, is Ellison's statement that "the values of my own people are neither 'white' nor 'black,' they are American. Nor can I see how they could be anything else, since we are a people who are involved in the texture of the American experience. And, indeed, today the most dramatic fight for American ideals is being sparked by black Americans" (*Shadow and Act,* p. 261).

The confrontation with the coiled serpent of history, the search for one's place in a radically altered world, was to proceed therefore in Western and American terms. But the black writers and liberation fighters of the fifties comprised a forthright and sophisticated group. Having seen the failings of the West, they refused to grant it their unfailing allegiance. If the pictures in the historical gallery all had a chiaroscuro quality, then these men and women decided they would seek out only the darker portions. They would attempt to articulate something uniquely black in the overall exhibit. Martin Luther King, for example, with deft and brilliant strokes, brought the black church into the freedom struggle, combined its doctrines and sanctions with the Eastern teachings of Mahatma Gandhi, and triggered an upheaval whose effects are still visible in America. Through intelligence tempered with what Ellison calls "Negro American style," King placed the civil rights worker in the moral vanguard of the modern world. And with several technically flawless and sweeping essays, James Baldwin established his credentials in a world company of writers.

It is worth pursuing the example of Baldwin to observe how his strategies differ from those of his immediate predecessors and from those of a long line of black spokesmen. Baldwin argues that slavery in America and the white cultural impulses that sanctioned it have yielded a society unwilling to go beyond fixed categories. This social world is bound together by "legend, myth, coercion"; its citizens fear that without such a bond they will be "hurled into that void" where, "like the earth before the word was spoken, the foundations of society are hidden" (*Notes,* p. 20). Though there are echoes of the storefront preacher here, Baldwin is actually championing a bold existential individualism on the part of the man of words. The "void" is identified as the self. Only by descending into the chaos of the self will the artist be able to fulfill his mission. Out of the wordless anarchy there, he speaks the new, presocial word that brings insight into the world. The writer, therefore, is a person who exists outside those confining social and linguistic categories that reduce all men to the "bloodless dimensions of a guy named Joe" (*Notes,* p. 20). The propositions here constitute a form of transcendent idealism that led to Baldwin's quarrel with black protest writers like Richard Wright and Chester Himes. Protest writing, Baldwin argues, accepts the harsh, grating, meaningless language that society metes out for its public discussions of ethnic minorities. Such writing is, therefore, unable to move beyond an exclusively social arena. It serves merely to confirm society's uniformed views of the problems that the writing seeks to address. The creations of an "honest" writer, by contrast, take as their subject the private self—the void from which the tides of history flow. And the language of the private self is poetic, analytical, asocial.

Baldwin's aesthetics represent a new departure. They allow him to admit candidly that when he found himself excluded from a Western heritage by the category "Negro" (or "nigger," as he states it with vehemence), he hated not only white people but also blacks. Since society provided no meaningful terms for his own experiences, he found himself stymied as a writer. Like Caliban, he had become articulate only to find that he was expected to curse. Instead of falling victim to this expectation, however, he chose to steal the sacred fires of the West. He appropriated the "white centuries" and moved beyond society altogether.

The picture is one of the black artist as intellectual rebel. As formulated by Baldwin, it is a new representation in the black American literary tradition and leads, ultimately, to a kind of theology of art. The black writer's possibilities include more than becoming simply a literate and troubling presence who articulates what seem on a surface view to be publicly sanctioned Western ideals. His potentialities are, in an almost frighteningly literal sense, infinite. For Baldwin, the claims of literature itself—as a separate sphere of endeavor—take precedence over all social or political concerns because the business of the writer is "revelation." Baldwin's ideal black spokesman, who is "socially responsible" to neither white nor black America, is an order of magnitude away from the autobiographical representations of Douglass and Washington. Of his speech at Nantucket, Douglass said: "It was a severe cross, and I took it up reluctantly." The black spokesman whom Baldwin envisions, however, feels a respectable ease in Zion because he is not concerned to take up any socially sanctioned gods, causes, or categories. Instead, he is himself a god.

Baldwin's Western-ness, then, is no simple matter. He cannot be easily categorized as "integrationist" or "assimilationist," since he is racing "with all deliberate speed" to escape society. He does say, "Most of them [black Americans] care nothing whatever about race. They want only their proper place in the sun and the right to be left alone, like any other citizen of the republic" (*Notes*, p. 27). He knows, however, that his own desires are more extensive. He is dedicated to a truth that lies within the self. Given the remarks on autobiography in the previous chapter, Baldwin's commitment could be described as intensely American. But its import seems to escape such an easy generalization. Baldwin's was a forced rather than a voluntary exile from society. It was almost an act of black criminality, as defined by the West. For Baldwin both stole an artistic heritage and insisted on employing it to destroy the prevailing American social fabric. By working inward, through an autobiographical recall grounded on a firm notion of the self's dominion (and a fine precision of language), he strove to shatter the taboos and clichés that ensured cohesiveness and complacency in the white world.

Yet some have assumed that Baldwin slavishly courted a Western muse and wished to become indistinguishable from white Americans. Nothing could be farther from the truth, as a view of his 1956 novel, *Giovanni's Room,* illustrates.[7] When the book opens, its white protagonist stands naked in front of a mirror on the day that his lover, Giovanni, is to be executed. In the novel's present, the white hero does absolutely nothing. His reflections on the past reveal that he has seldom done much more. His life has been one of "a wanderer, an adventurer, rocking through the world unanchored" (*Giovanni's Room,* p. 84), and his expressed guilt and anxiety are reduced to the following terms by one of the work's villains: "just an American boy, after all, doing things in France which you would not dare to at home"(*Giovanni's Room,* p. 142). Though it contains resonant passages reflecting the white intellectual climate of the fifties, *Giovanni's Room* scarcely seems the work of a writer enchanted by the white West. The cast does not include a single character who can face the dreadful revelations of the self. Above all, the novel seems to offer a scathingly revisionist view of what it means to be a white American male in the modern world. Certainly Baldwin has spoken of it in these terms.[8]

The idealistic aesthetics and the Promethean flare with which Baldwin evades society illustrate the sophisticatedness of the black response during the fifties. The kind of spiritual, even theological, transcendentalism that lies at the core of his and Martin Luther King's projections, however, does not complete the inventory. Richard Wright approached the facts of Western-ness in very secular terms. In *White Man, Listen!* he describes the disruption occasioned by colonialism and slavery: "In sum, a kind of void, emotional and psychological in nature, existed in the social structure, and only a few . . . seemed aware of it" (p. 116).[9] The "void" for Wright is not spiritual; it is social. His focus is the recently liberated nations of Asia and Africa and the urgent problems confronting them. The most pressing difficulty is what Wright describes in *Pagan Spain* as "a muddy residue of irrational paganism."[10] The dogmas of ancient religions and the emotional dependence they foster continue even after the withdrawal of the colonizers. They prevent the masses from moving into the modern world. Wright is unsparing in his condemnation of such retarding spiritual behaviors: "the teeming religions gripping the minds and consciousness of Asians and Africans offend me. I can conceive no identification with such mystical visions of life that freeze millions in static degradation, no matter how emotionally satisfying such degradation seems to those who wallow in it" (*White Man, Listen!* pp. 48–49). He proposes Western rationalism as a desirable alternative to these static patterns of belief. If Baldwin would make a heaven in hell's despite, Wright steers strictly by the compass of reason.

Although he feels that Western rationalism was a historical accident of Calvin's and Luther's efforts to bring about spiritual reform in Europe, Wright asserts that once allowed into the world, this rationality led to the Enlightenment and to the subsequent growth of science and industry. The most significant aspect of the advanced technological state, according to Wright, is man's emotional independence, his freedom from cloying ties of custom and tradition. The liberated, secular personality becomes, therefore, Wright's sounding board for a people's commitment to modernity.

The freest men in all the world are those who compose the "tragic élite"—former colonial subjects who have been educated in the West and now serve as leaders of emergent colored nations. Since they have been cut off from their traditional cultures and excluded from a natural, organic participation in Western civilization, they see things from "another and third point of view" (*White Man, Listen!* p. 48). The most advanced among this group are artists and scholars. Their temperaments have conditioned them to grasp the world in enlightened terms:

> It has been almost only among Asians and Africans of an artistic stamp . . . that I've found a sense of the earth belonging to and being the natural home of, all the men inhabiting it, an attitude that went well beyond skin color, races, parties, classes, and nations . . . . Among some Asian-African scholastic circles, I found that Western scientific thought had encouraged some rare men toward a healthy skepticism not only of Christianity, but toward all traditional ideas. Striking advances in the realms of anthropology and Freudian psychology have stressed not as much the old-time diversities among men that the colonials and nineteenth-century scientists loved to insist upon, but the remarkable and growing body of evidence of the basic emotional kinship, empirically established, of all men and of all races . . . . Today many of the scholars of Asia and Africa (a minority, to be sure, for I've found that psychological facts do not sit well upon the mentalities of oppressed people!) are beginning to feel a lessening of distance between themselves and the Western world. [*White Man, Listen!* pp. 25–26]

The corollary to this description of the scholar-artist is the following characterization of art: "I believe that art has its own autonomy, a self-sufficiency that extends beyond, and independent of, the sphere of political or priestly power or sanction" (*White Man, Listen!* p. 50).

Rationality, in short, leads the Third World scholar-artist to question all traditional barriers and distinctions. Emotional independence not only allows him to move closer to a Western sensibility, but also enables him to project a future world where men and women will be united by the common bond of reason. Translated to the United States, Wright's view forecasts the disappearance of black literature as a distinct body of expression. The increased Westernization of America—reflected in the Supreme Court decision of 1954—means that blacks will move toward a commonality of experience with whites (*White Man, Listen!* pp. 103–4). When this occurs, black literature will merge into the larger mainstream. Such speculations are logical outgrowths of Wright's proposition that the artist possesses an informed sense of mankind's "emotional kinship." Segregation in the United States has acted as an implacable obstacle to such unity, and black writers have ceaselessly protested its divisions. When it is removed, however, the social situation will become conducive to an alliance of all men, black and white alike. The black writer's work will, in turn, be less strident, reflecting the common ideals of a changing world.

There are several striking aspects to these formulations by Wright. First, there is their intense, rational secularism. In his 1945 autobiography, *Black Boy,* Wright pays great homage to the emotions; the self revealed by the work is one which continually chafes against restrictions on the life of feeling. Although it is true that even in *Black Boy* Wright seems to view a full human emotional development as a means to Western civilization, I think the autobiography in itself profoundly accentuates the means rather than the end. In his later books, however, Wright is a devout advocate for reason. One explanation is that having freed himself by the 1950s from those tempting, even sensual, ties extended by family and religion, Wright welcomed both his own emotional freedom and the rationality of the modern state.

The second thing to note is Wright's firm discipleship to the West. The same West that accepted racism as an ersatz religion is exonerated by Wright because the central historic fact of colonialism and slavery, in his view, has been the advent of rationality. This represents a clear objectification. Having progressed from a southern, peasant mode of existence to a Western frame of reference, Wright projects this movement onto the world at large. As he subjectively glories in his own journey, he also praises the efforts of those who will bring the masses of Asia and Africa to the peaks of Western consciousness. He even sanctions the use of Western methods in order to achieve this goal. "Yes," he says, "Sukarno, Nehru, Nasser and others will necessarily use quasi-dictatorial methods to hasten the process of social evolution and to establish order in their lands" (*White Man, Listen!* p. 65). And at the conclusion of *Black Power,* he advocates the most stringent methods of government control in Ghana.[11] Wright's views, then, led to a tolerance for neocolonialism. Black faces replace white ones in his picture of newly emergent nations, but the means of governance remain the same. This marks but another example of that alliance with the supposed ideals of whites that we have witnessed in the work of other writers.

The third striking element in Wright is the view of the artist that appears in his later works. In "Blueprint for Negro Writing" (1937), he champions the writer's standing shoulder to shoulder with the black migratory workers whose folk expression offers both social insight and literary themes for the creative artist.[12] But in *White Man, Listen!* the writer stands shoulder to shoulder with the Western white man, glorying not in the "forms of things unknown" (black folk forms), but in the decreasing distance between himself and those of the West who share his conviction of mankind's essential unity. Wright's conception of the sweep of contemporary history enabled him to place his faith in the secular state as a perfectible model for the future. As society moves continuously into accord with the writer's almost inherent sense of mankind's oneness, he has no choice but to celebrate the emotional independence motivating this progress. His mode of expression must be social, secular, and Western because, as such, it reflects the most precious legacy of contemporary history. What Wright implies is that the black writer—a man released from all loyalties by the sheer weight of historical circumstances—is a radical outsider who serves as a guide to the future. Like the current advanced technological state of which he is part, he both exemplifies and serves as a harbinger of the Western life yet to come. Finally, the conceptual scheme that Wright's propositions imply is not terribly unlike Booker T. Washington's.

These last speculations are qualified, however, by two later novels—*The Long Dream* and *Savage Holiday*. *The Long Dream* deals with the cramped, stultifying, segregated life of the American South. In a number of instances, the narrative assumes the tone of expression—fierce, irreverent, despairingly sensual—that Wright sees as a distinct manner of speaking of the black migratory worker. "I'm an American!" thunders Zeke to Rex (Fishbelly) Tucker and his companions. "Nigger," responds Sam:

> "You're dreaming. You ain't no American! You live Jim Crow. Don't you ride Jim Crow trains? Jim Crow busses? Don't you go to Jim Crow restaurants? Jim Crow schools? Jim Crow churches? Ain't your undertaking parlors and graveyards Jim Crow? Try and git a room in that West End Hotel where Chris is working and them white folk'll lynch your black ass to hell and gone! You can't live like no American! And you ain't African neither! So what is you? Nothing! Just nothing!"[13]

The morally impoverished world that Fishbelly discovers as he grows up confirms Sam's statement. The Mississippi black belt, the novel's setting, hardly seems a place where blacks and whites will merge and share an integrated American literature. It seems probable that blues heard in the novel's Grove Bar and Dance Hall, sermons like that preached at Tyree Tucker's funeral, and resonant condemnations such as Sam's will remain the norm. Wright's notion of the tragic élite, moreover, is contradicted by Tyree's assertion that "there ain't no *low* niggers and *high* niggers for white folks. We all the same to them, except when they can get something out of us" (*The Long Dream,* p. 231).

In *Savage Holiday* the complexion of the cast changes to white, and Wright attempts a psychological portrayal of modern bureaucratic man. Erskine Fowler, an insurance executive forced into retirement, finds himself nude and locked out of his apartment on a Sunday morning. His subsequent thoughts and actions compose a nightmarish array. When he finally hands himself over to the police and confesses that he is responsible for the deaths of his neighbor and her son, even he feels his motivations are unlikely: "How could he ever explain that a daydream buried under the rigorous fiats of duty had been called forth from its thirty-six-year-old grave by a woman called Mabel Blake, and that that taunting dream had so overwhelmed him with a sense of guilt compounded of a reality which was strange and alien and which he loathed, but which, at the same time, was astonishingly familiar to him: a guilty dream which he had wanted to disown and forget, but which he had had to reenact in order to make its memory and reality clear to him!"[14]

Taken together, *Savage Holiday* and *The Long Dream* represent the sober, unfulfilled efforts of a chronically skeptical black writer. They qualify immeasurably Wright's ringing praises for the West. Tyree and Fishbelly are no more representative of black men who will lead the masses into the future than Erskine Fowler is an example of the free white secular personality. The Western white man's religion of racism, it would seem, had left enduring marks on Wright. He who had sanctioned neocolonialism, issued proclamations of liberation, and had visions of a unified world found himself, in his declining years, portraying the bondage and divisions of the past. His Western-ness, therefore, is a position of hopeful ambivalence rather than of firm persuasion. He was too aware of the large, ungraceful failings of the West—having felt them dramatically in his own life—to translate the predictions of *White Man, Listen!* into utopian creative scenes where race, class, and religion no longer mattered. And in this respect, his work is far removed from Washington's *Up from Slavery*.

Somewhere between Baldwin's almost sacred characterizations of art and the secular view of Wright stands the work of Ralph Ellison. Although Ellison feels that a writer's work—a novel in particular—is social in derivation and effect, he also specifies an idealistic middle road for art and the artist. In order to move from his direct experiences and the traditions of his culture to a finished work of art, the writer journeys through the mediating realm of "literature." Ellison's own creative endeavors illustrate this progression:

> I use folklore in my work not because I am Negro, but because writers like Eliot and Joyce made me conscious of the literary value of my folk inheritance .... the Negro is also an heir of the human experience which is literature, and this might well be more important to him than his living folk tradition .... for the novelist, of any cultural or racial identity, his form is his greatest freedom. [*Shadow and Act*, p. 70]

Ellison, however, does not devalue black American folklore. In "The Art of Fiction: An Interview," he says:

> Through the very process of slavery came the building of the United States. Negro folklore, evolving within a larger culture

> which regarded it as inferior, was an especially courageous expression. It announced the Negro's willingness to trust his own experience, his own sensibilities as to the definition of reality, rather than allow his masters to define these crucial matters for him. [*Shadow and Act*, p. 173]

He is not seeking to underrate folklife, therefore, when he states the importance of literary tradition. Rather he is attempting to emphasize his conviction (somewhat similar to Baldwin's) that the imaginative realm is one of transcendental value. Black folklore—and, indeed, all other aspects of the writer's personal and social experience—must be "raised" to the level of "art" before it can achieve its most important meanings. On this plane, traditional social distinctions disappear ("That phenomenon which Malraux calls the 'Imaginary Museum' draws no color line," *Shadow and Act*, p. 258), and all men wage the same battle for freedom. Whether it is called the "artistic heritage," "Imaginary Museum," or "literary tradition," Ellison's via media appears remarkably similar to Baldwin's "self." It is a domain unburdened by restrictive categories, and it yields clarity, insight, freedom, and form.

But if this characterization makes Ellison's point of view seem a simple attenuation of Baldwin's, it is important to note that at other moments Ellison sounds like an ardent social reformer:

> People rationalize what they shun or are incapable of dealing with; these superstitions and their rationalizations become ritual as they govern behavior. The rituals become social forms, and it is one of the functions of the artist to recognize them and raise them to the level of art. . . . Take the "Battle Royal" passage in my novel [*Invisible Man*], where the boys are blindfolded and forced to fight each other for the amusement of the white observers. This is a vital part of behavior pattern in the South, which both Negroes and whites thoughtlessly accept. It is ritual in preservation of caste lines, a keeping of taboo to appease the gods and ward off bad luck. . . . This passage . . . I did not have to invent; the patterns were already there in society, so that all I had to do was present them in a broader context of meaning. [*Shadow and Act*, p. 175]

Like Wright's scholar-artist, Ellison's ideal writer provides an index of meanings for society. He possesses, that is to say, an inescapable social responsibility. Commenting on his search for artistic form, Ellison says:

> I found myself turning to our classical nineteenth-century novelists . . . . I came to believe that the writers of that period took a much greater responsibility for the condition of democracy and, indeed, their works were imaginative projections of the conflicts within the human heart which arose when the sacred principles of the Constitution and the Bill of Rights clashed with the practical exigencies of human greed and fear, hate and love. Naturally I was attracted to these writers as a Negro. Whatever they thought of my people per se, in their imaginative economy the Negro symbolized both the man lowest down and the mysterious, underground aspect of human personality. In a sense the Negro was the gauge of the human condition as it waxed and waned in our democracy. [*Shadow and Act,* pp. 112–13]

What is notable here is the position of the black experience at the center of the writer's moral concerns. Just as Wright placed his faith in a Western emotional independence, so Ellison endorses Western democracy as a framework that promises a harmonious future coexistence between blacks and whites. The inequities of the black situation act as barriers to this goal. And the committed American writer must clarify the condition of blacks before America can move closer to its "sacred principles." The world unity that Ellison projects, however, is quite different from Wright's. For Ellison, the black person does not surrender his identity and disappear into an undifferentiated Western mass. The black man or woman becomes, instead, a celebrated and unique part of American life. The general American-ness of the black experience, in other words, originates in, and remains qualified by, an enduring cultural particularity: "Nor are we interested in being anything other than *Negro* Americans . . . . The point of our struggle is to be both Negro and American and to bring about that condition in American society in which this would be possible" (*Shadow and Act,* pp. 261–62). For the black writer, this means a continuing emphasis on the "specific forms of humanity" defined by black folk materials at the same instant that he is preparing to enter the "imaginary museum" or, to put it another way, preserving sui generis semantic fields as he journeys over the American ground between heaven and Africa.

Ellison assumes that the artistic and social traditions conditioning his aesthetics are his "by right of birth." Unlike Baldwin, he feels no need to debate his legitimacy as a writer. His movement from the social to the imaginative domain, therefore, is one of calm certainty rather than of harried rebellion. Forten and Ellison thus seem to share a similar perspective on the "excellent laws and just government which we [blacks] now enjoy, in common, with every individual of the community." And though Ellison's writings share the 1950s optimism that prophesied world unity, they do not contain the urgent demand for a Western utopia that led to such striking contradictions for Wright. Ellison's work is that of a man speaking in tones of acceptance. But to categorize it merely as "assimilationist" is to do its author a disservice. For though his writings, at a number of points, present an illustration of the type of work Wright predicted from black writers, they also describe, in exact terms, a uniquely black experience, elucidating its stirring origins and the relationships it sustains to a complex surrounding culture. Perhaps it is his sharp sense of specifics within a large, fluid field that makes Ellison one of the most sophisticated spokesmen of the 1950s.

Mirroring the concerns of major figures like Wright, Ellison, and Baldwin were two writers' conferences and two important creative works of the 1950s. On September 19, 1956, the Conference of Negro-African Writers and Artists opened in Paris. Assembled there were Western-educated artists who sought to initiate a dialogue with the West. The spirit of the affair, said Léopold Senghor, the Senegalese poet and diplomat, was one of a second Bandung. The dispossessed of the earth were coming together to evaluate and record their cultural contributions. Recognizing the uniqueness of their traditional arts, spokesmen from Africa, the Caribbean, and black America insisted on the need for a "cultural inventory" and for a coherent plan to perpetuate the black arts. The change of prospect signaled by such an agenda is unbelievable. To view the distance between Vassa's lonely attempts to make known the history of black captivity and the 1950s scene in Paris, where articulate black spokesmen from all points of the African diaspora joined together to recover their past, is to witness the incredibly brief maturation of the black writer. Reaching back over the years and across the disrupted spaces, the black spokesmen at Paris sought ways to make known the journey in all its vivid details.

The ironical restriction of the conference was that political issues were forbidden: a number of participants were from still colonized territories. Nonetheless, the fact that men like Alioune Diop, Aimé Césaire, John Price Mars, George Lamming, Richard Wright and others came together in the name of "Negro-African" art testified to the felt freedoms of the 1950s. It also revealed the new sense of African origins characteristic of many diasporic writers during the decade. And while Baldwin archly hints in *Nobody Knows My Name* that nothing of significance transpired at the conference,[15] the tenor of the affair was one of individuals boldly facing the responsibilities of their new historical position and awareness. Moreover, the event led to the establishment of the American Society of African Culture, which held the first Conference of Negro Writers in March of 1959.

The theme of this event was "The Negro Writer and His Roots," and it recapitulated the concerns of Paris and highlighted the problematical role of the black writer in America. For although the participants repeatedly expressed their hopes for democracy, they also cautioned against an unthinking acceptance of the American artistic mainstream.[16] Samuel Allen, Loften Mitchell, Julian Mayfield, and John O. Killens all warned that the black writer might be better served by analyzing his relationship to Africa, Negritude, or a southern, agrarian "homeland" than by adopting a dominant white literary tradition. While most suggested that black protest writing was démodé, no one recommended a smooth compromise with existing American literary standards. Instead, they called for a serious questioning of prevailing aesthetic criteria.[17] And they stated their indisputable alliance with the colored peoples of the world. Mitchell wrote:

> The rising tide of African nationalism and the uprooting of colonialism have brought reality crashing against the lies of history. The restless stirring in our own southland is from a people turning *towards* their roots, not seeking to lose their newly found identity.... While it is true that American Negroes are arguing for integration—and that they have too long been influenced by a white majority, the majority of the present-day, shrinking world happens to be colored.[18]

Although the conference rehearsed familiar themes and voiced familiar hopes, it also introduced into an American context the themes, concerns, and allegiances of a rising Third World. In its proceedings one finds foreshadowings, if not direct statements, of some of the issues that have engaged subsequent black authors. Like Ellison and Wright, the participants knew they were in a Western arena. But they also realized that the battle to be waged in this arena was for autonomy: "The mainstream of American arts and letters, as we have seen, falls somewhat short of reflecting the Negro with dignity and complete psychological integrity. To think merely of joining that stream or to think of our creative efforts simply as part of that stream would mean to fall to a substantial degree under the influence of its direction and to perpetuate in part its cultural prototype."[19] Here we have black writers who have sighted other lands and know that America may not offer the only ground of inspiration for their work. The possibility of new allegiances is dramatically posed in most of their statements.

If the Paris and New York conferences paralleled the work of Wright and Ellison, there was at least one celebrated work of the fifties that was more fully in accord with Baldwin's aesthetics. Melvin Tolson's *Libretto for the Republic of Liberia*, which subjects the history of the ancient and modern world to the compressed ambiguities of the "New Poetry," is a text that turns inward to the private spaces of the self. Written as a commemorative epic for the Liberian centennial, the poem is the end-product of an artist who had appropriated the literary language of "white centuries." Its author seems so engrossed in a play of wit and learning that Africa becomes little more than the central image around which his allusions coalesce. It might be argued that substantial effort and some attention to the work's more than one hundred notes have their rewards for the reader. But the following excerpt reveals the difficulties one encounters in making such a case:

> *"Ecce homo!"*
> the blind men cowled in azure rant
> before the Capitol
> between the Whale and Elephant
> Where no longer stands Diogenes' hearse
> readied for the ebony mendicant
> nor weeping widow Europe with her hands
> making the multitudinous seas incarnadine . . .[20]

Perhaps the game is not worth the candle. Each of the poem's gestures seems to seek the vast stolen stores of the West as a final reference. The work becomes a world accessible only to those who are willing to labor at an inventory of these Western treasures.

Suspended between the conferences' demands for a revised artistic representation of black experience and the allusively self-contained verse of Tolson stands the careful realism of Lorraine Hansberry's *A Raisin in the Sun*. The first play by a black woman to reach Broadway (it opened March 11, 1959), *Raisin* captures the admixture of optimism and reserve that marks the fifties. While Walter Lee Younger, the play's protagonist, has dreams of his imminent success as an American businessman, and while Beneatha (Walter's sister) and Asagai (her African boyfriend) share reveries of a glorious age in Africa, Lena Younger clings to a common-sense view of life that holds everyone in check. As a descendant of five generations of slaves and sharecroppers, Lena knows that some of life's battles are more important than others. Her first priority is to shatter the restrictive mentality—that white cultural hegemony—that seeks to relegate blacks to the cramped ghettos of the world. She intends to have a home in a white neighborhood, and she holds all her children to a line that will take them there. Meanwhile, Africa and black aspirations toward the white world (masterfully satirized in George Murchison) will have to wait. Walter's "manhood" resides in his reluctant assent to his mother's vision. The play closes on moving day with the Youngers facing the perils (and the supposed benefits) of a white Chicago neighborhood.

Hansberry's work offers a fitting close to the decade. In its representation of a world in transition, it refuses to accept easy generalizations about either the past or the future. It is essentially the story of non-college-educated black men and women of older generations. Walter and his mother are confronting a brave new world with a traditional black American wisdom and dignity. They are people who have been in the storm so long that they are not easily undone by the first clear days. Their goals are as immediate as a physical departure from the slums of society. The symbolic freight of their move comes from the misty, enthusiastic, at times humorous dialogue between the youth of the cast. Walter, his wife Ruth, and his mother Lena are usually incredulous (or openly cynical) before these outpourings. Yet there is enough fire in Beneatha's convictions to stir up heated exchanges, and one has the feeling that the older characters will become as committed to the spirit of their flight from the ghetto as they are currently to its more tangible aspects. The mood is one of hope. The doubtful voyagers have still to see the landfall, but they are encouraged by prophecies of a brighter resting place yet to come.

A Raisin in the Sun's guarded attitude toward the future is in harmony with the breathless reaction of Ellison's protagonist. The elemental fact of Primus Provo's free papers is that they were drafted such a short time ago. The world has not yet stabilized around his liberation. Until it does, a variety of strategies must be explored by black spokesmen. The Western secularism of Wright, the transcendent idealism of Baldwin, and the democratic American-ness of Ellison are all efforts to state new terms for order after the black American writer has traveled to the center of the Western arena. At the center, he discovered that history does indeed have "many cunning passages." But he also found that he was not alone. A real Africa, awake and coming to full consciousness, existed, and throughout his own land black freedom fighters were insisting that the obstacles of the past would soon be overcome. The task, then, was not only to expose the false categories and aspirations of the past, but also to construct a dramatically new set of artistic and social norms suitable for a black world coming to birth.

4 In Our Own Time: The Florescence of Nationalism in the Sixties and Seventies

The Alabama night settled on a small shack at the edge of Selma. Sitting by a fire, made hastily to keep off the chill, a young civil rights worker recalled a "hot, late summer day" in Wilcox County. Surrounded by deputies, lines of black people were waiting to vote. Suddenly:

> A white man leaped from the rank of deputies into the midst of the students. Fists clenched in the air, he shook a writhing, green snake .... The man tried to force the snake into a boy's mouth. When the youngster gritted his teeth and pursed his lips, the man laughed and tried to stuff his sickness down other throats .... When, desperately, a victim threw out an arm to protect himself, knocking the snake to the street, the man grew wide-eyed with shock and indignation. Two of the deputies came dashing forward. They led the Negro to a squad car. At the stationhouse, Sheriff Jim Clark's deputies charged him with assault and jailed him.[1]

The black man's jailing is less striking than his physical reaction to the white man's "sickness." The intensity of that hot southern moment, with its image of blacks passively waiting, unprotected by the laws of the region, lies in the sudden raising of a black man's arm. Amazed, perhaps terrified, the white law moves into action. The frame might be frozen as a pointed comment on the 1960s.

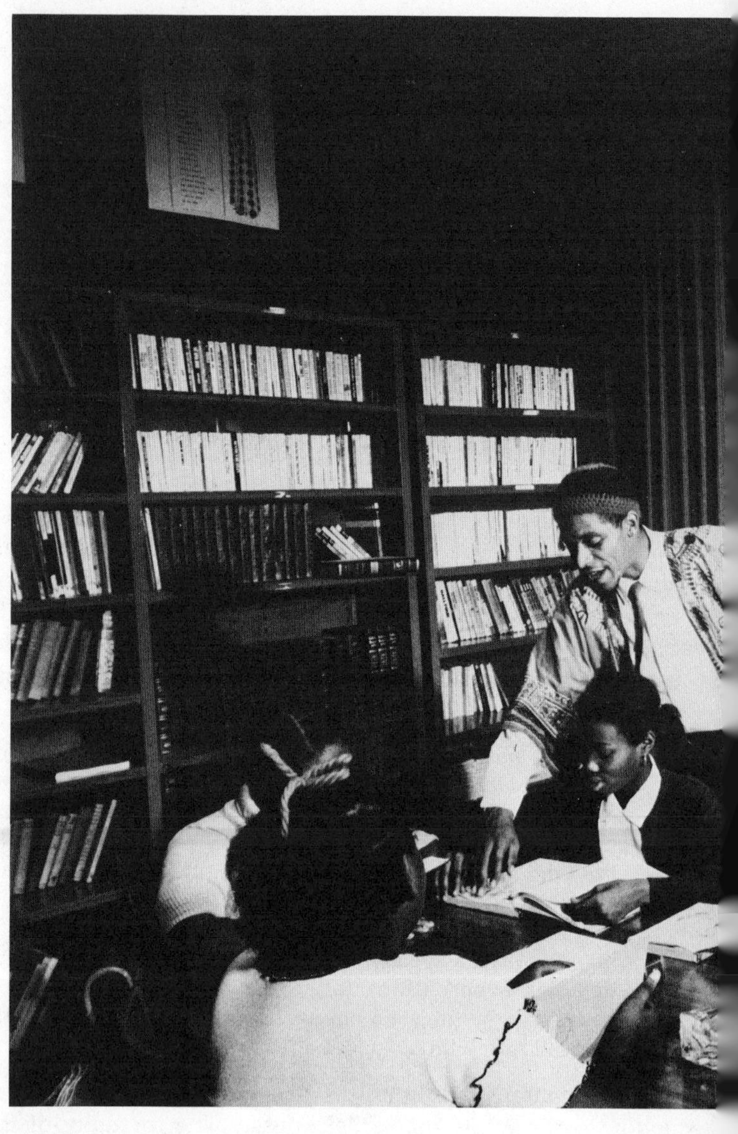

During the decade, blacks moved decisively away from the Christian humility and Gandhian forbearance that marked the strategy of Martin Luther King. And as their voices became more strident, their actions more daringly aggressive, the police forces of America were converted from domestic law enforcement agencies into what seemed heavily armed military regiments. It was not blacks alone for whom these forces were upgraded. Young whites also became vociferous and aggressive as America's involvement in the Vietnamese War increased. By the fall of 1963, it was clear to many that the optimistic mood of the fifties had been replaced by one of violence and despair. In that year, Medgar Evers, John F. Kennedy, and four young black Birmingham, Alabama, Sunday-school worshipers were murdered. The violence of their deaths was not singular; it was simply the most publicly lamented. Combined with this publicized violence, in the North and South alike, was an ongoing hostility that threatened to destroy the nation. The Johnson administration's passage of a civil rights bill in 1964 and launching of a "War on Poverty" served to channel some of the restless energies of the sixties. But by 1966, both blacks and whites knew that America was destined for extremes. Stokely Carmichael, president of the Student Nonviolent Coordinating Committee, urged blacks to substitute "Black Power" for civil rights in their demands. And in many of those urban concentrations of blacks in the North and the West his injunction was heeded. The new phrase "Black Power!" rang out with the sound of gunfire and the rumble of tanks that characterized ghetto uprisings. In 1968, Huey Newton and Bobby Seale, two young black men from Oakland, California, heightened the conflict, which had already reached near hysterical proportions with the assassination of Martin Luther King on April 4.

Newton and Seale organized the Black Panther Party as a group whose avowed intentions included the bearing of arms and the destruction of the white world's power over the inner city. Cries for "Black Power" changed to fierce calls for "Black Revolution." On college campuses, young blacks adopted the posture and rhetoric of revolt and moved to close down these institutions if their demands for black studies programs, increased black enrollment, and more black faculty were not met. Meanwhile, black communities continued to erupt in civil disorder, and thousands of young war protesters were clubbed into retreat during the Democratic political convention in the summer of 1968. Later that year, Richard Nixon came to power with the rallying cry, "Law and Order."

The last two years of the decade and the beginning of the seventies found black men and women throughout America with their arms raised in the closed-fist salute of Black Power-Black Revolution. Many had more than fists to clutch; they had sophisticated weapons. But picking up the gun did little good. The Black Panthers, and virtually every other American radical group, were effectively eliminated by a government-sanctioned wave of repression that might be equated with the violence directed at organized labor earlier in this century. When the Vietnamese War drew to an agonizing conclusion, talk of the imminent overthrow of white America had waned. Those signs of a raised black American consciousness—the Afro hairstyle, the dashiki, and the tricolored black nationalist flag—had begun to disappear. Soon the country at large had to contend with the despair of Watergate.

The nature of black people's actions during the sixties and early seventies, however, left them more cause for pride than despair. Their arms had been raised in a gesture of unconditional refusal, and many had granted their allegiance to black nationalist doctrines so convincingly advocated by a man like Malcolm X. It was paradoxical that those who had so recently come into contact with the writhing history of the West felt compelled to reject it. It was as though possession of what Wright called "a vocabulary of history" gave blacks precisely the terms they needed to protect themselves, to knock the serpent of the Western historical aberrations into the street. Or, to state this in another way, it was as though blacks after a long pilgrimage had arrived at the Western city only to find it stricken with plague, or caught in the lurid flames of its destruction.

As an alternative to the sickness and death at hand, blacks proposed a new nation founded on distinctively black and African elements that had never been allowed within the boundaries of the city. Rather than study the torturous coils of the dying, they sought to bring forth new life. Black writers were in the forefront of this effort. And no canon reflects the process more accurately than that of Amiri Baraka (né LeRoi Jones).

Baraka began writing as what he calls a "schwartze Bohemien." The mode is caricatured in *Preface to a Twenty-Volume Suicide Note:*

> They laught,
> and religion was something
> he fount in coffee shops, by God.
> It's not that I got enything
> against cotton, nosiree, by God
> It's just that . . .
>   Man lookatthatblonde
>   whewee![2]

The early poetry is sometimes a verse of "maudlin nostalgia / that comes on / like terrible thoughts about death" (*Preface,* p. 17). At other moments, it approximates a game of surreal self-display like that of the speaker in "Scenario IV":

> The motion of the mind! Smooth; I jiggle
> & clack stomping one foot & the clothesline swings.
> Fabulei Verwachsenses. Ripping this one off
> in a series of dramatic half-turns I learned
> many years ago in the orient; Baluba:
> "The power to cloud men's minds" etc., which
> I'm sure you must have heard about, doddle-doo
> & then I'm sittin in this red chair, humming,
> feet still pecking at the marble floor . . .
>
> [*Preface,* pp. 22–23]

Its prevailing tone is one of elegant despair tempered by an inclination for the grotesque and the absurd. There are instances, however, when the poet brings clear focus to what he describes as the "mosaic of disorder I own" (*Preface,* p. 27). In the following lines, for example, he sets forth images that are central to his canon:

> Emotion. Words
> Waste, No clear delight.
> No light under my fingers. The room, The
> walls, silent & deadly. Not
> Music.
>
> [*Preface,* p. 32]

This is a rendering of the sealed consciousness, the mind in its silences and the body bereft of touch.

The "room" appears time and again in Baraka's poetry. Its structures—walls and window—may be set by the sea or on the wet grounds of a landscape that overlooks the waters. The person occupying the room joins a company characterized as "isolate / land creatures in a wet unfriendly world" (*Preface,* p. 18). But even though the poet feels cut off in his distances where "not even cars . . . are real" (*Preface,* p. 38), and even though he feels "barely human" (*Preface,* p. 35), he is still capable of sharp insights that bring some understanding of his own and society's plight. His character as an artist is not entirely solipsistic:

> What are
> influences?
> A green truck
> wet & glowing, seance
> of ourselves, elegy for the sea
> at night, my flesh
> a woman's at the fingertips
> soft white increased coolness
> from the dark
> sea.
>
> [*Preface,* p. 36]

The sea of everyday existence—including the mundane sight of a truck or the love of a woman—invades and shapes the room's spaces. Moreover, the poet realizes that what keeps him from turning outward to the world of flesh and influences is a kind of Western enervation:

> No use for beauty
> collapsed, with moldy breath
> done in. Insidious weight

of cankered dreams. Tiresias'
weathered cock.

[*Preface*, pp. 24–25]

There are at least two adequate readings for the title of the poem in which these lines appear, "Way out West." Caught in his hermetic room, the poet can still offer a critique of the outside environment and recognize his need for a broader range. His despair, in any case, may derive from a definition of writing that sees the poem as

A
turning away . . . .
from what
it was
had moved
us . . .
A
Madness.

[*Preface*, p. 40]

Clearly, influences would be irrelevant to a canon that conformed perfectly to such a view. Furthermore, the individual poem might be reduced to the experience of "the spent lover / smelling his fingers" (*Preface*, p. 41). In a sense, the definition itself and the fact that "nothing is happening to me (in this world)" (*Preface*, p. 27) are conditions of what the poet considers his own inescapable American-ness:

African blues
does not know me. Their steps, in sands
of their own
land. A country
in black & white, newspapers
blown down pavements
of the world. Does
not feel
What I am

. . . .

. . . Africa
is a foreign place. You are
as any other sad man here
american.

[*Preface*, p. 47]

The prospect is not unlike that sanctioned by Baraka's predecessors who chose the middle ground of the United States as their ultimate point of reference. The lines are from "Notes for a Speech," the final poem in *Preface*. They seem to promise little success for the poet who says:

> I am thinking
> of a dance. One I could
> invent, if there
> were music . . .
>
> [*Preface*, p. 32]

The jaded world of *Preface*, with its bare glimmerings of hope, is an impressionistic reflection of the external reality with which Baraka found himself involved during the early sixties. He says in "Cuba Libre," a 1960 essay from *Home:*

> The most severe condemnation of American leaders by the American intellectual is that they are "bumblers," unintelligent but well-meaning clowns. But we do not realize how much of the horrible residue of these paid liars is left in our heads. . . . We reject the blatant, less dangerous lie, in favor of the subtle subliminal lie, which is more dangerous because we feel we are taking an intelligent stance, not being had. . . . There is a certain hopelessness about our attitude that can even be condoned. The environment sickens. The young intellectual living in the United States inhabits an ugly void. He cannot use what is around him, neither can he revolt against it. . . . Revolution in this country of "due process of law" would be literally impossible. Whose side would you be on? The void of being killed by what is in this country and not knowing what is outside of it.[3]

The context of this assessment, as one might gather from the essay's title, is America's relationship to the Third World, that new sector of existence that was such a rejuvenating sighting for the black writers of the fifties. Baraka insists that no one in the United States has an informed view of the world's emerging nations. The media, moreover, propagate nothing but lies about the new people who are coming to power and establishing a more humane way of life. Trapped in the isolationist environment produced by this state of affairs, Baraka felt that he had to cultivate an apolitical realm of higher ideas. When confronted by a radical Mexican delegate to the Cuban liberation celebration who tells him of America's "irrationality" and blindness, he responds, "Look, why jump on me? I understand what you're saying. I'm in complete agreement with you. I'm a poet . . . . what can I do? I write, that's all, I'm not even interested in politics" (*Home*, p.42).

But he soon transcended this void of social and political indifference. He did so through a discovery of two overriding aspects of American life that keep the country at stalemate. The first was liberalism; the second was the tokenism which this philosophy inspired:

> It is just this group of amateur social theorists, American Liberals, who have done most throughout American history to insure the success of tokenism. Whoever has proposed whatever particular social evasion or dilution—to whatever ignominious end—it is usually the liberal who gives that lie the greatest lip service. They, liberals, are people with extremely heavy consciences and almost nonexistent courage. Too little is always enough. And it is always the *symbol* that appeals to them most . . . . for them "moderation" is a kind of religious catch phrase that they are wont to mumble on street corners even alone late at night. [*Home*, pp. 76–77]

The consequences of what Baraka calls the "Liberal/Missionary syndrome" include a falsification of history, a perpetuation of the myth of progress as a way of salving consciences, and the deluding of subjugated peoples through the creation and doling out of tokens. These all work against what Baraka considers primary—man's freedom. White American liberals and their middle-class advocates, by cleverly subverting the legitimate aspiration of the masses, simply stand in the way of any real movement in society. This is contrary, Baraka asserts, to the natural state of human existence: "A man is either free or he is not. There cannot be any apprenticeship for freedom" (*Home*, pp. 80–81). The statement is a clear reflection of the chant, "Freedom Now!" that was welling up throughout black America. It stands in marked contrast to Vassa's and Forten's methodically detailed accounts of the skills and habits blacks must acquire before they can enjoy the life of free men. It is almost as though Baraka, with a stroke of the pen, had jettisoned the ideal of blacks' joining the larger society through a slow and torturous fitness campaign for equality.

This revision of ideals heralded a new stage in Baraka's work. In "Black Is a Country," he says, "What I am driving at is the fact that to me the Africans, Asians, and Latin Americans who are news today because of their nationalism, *i.e.*, the militant espousal of the doctrine of serving one's own people's interests before those of a foreign country, *e.g.*, the United States, are exactly the examples the Black man in this country should use in his struggle for *independence*" (*Home*, p. 84). The clear alliance of the black American condition and that of Third World nations is not simply a remarking of similarities; it is a strategic identification. In other words, Baraka is not simply stating that all of the world's oppressed peoples share a common predicament. He is asserting that black Americans must declare a sovereign state and accept nationalism as a way of achieving their complete liberation. He is patently aware that this view runs counter to more moderate positions of his day: "the struggle moves to make certain that no man has the right to dictate the life of another man. The struggle is not simply for 'equality,' or 'better jobs,' or 'better schools,' and the rest of those half-hearted liberal cliches; it is to completely *free* the black man from the domination of the white man. Nothing else .... The Negro's struggle in America is only a microcosm of the struggle of the new countries all over the world" (*Home*, pp. 84–85). At the same time, Baraka is still able to suggest that whites and blacks in America share a common destiny: "America is as much a black country as a white one. The lives and destinies of the white American are bound up inextricably with those of the black American, even though the latter has been forced for hundreds of years to inhabit the lonely country of black" (*Home*, p. 85).

Baraka's endorsement of black separatism in America was not so firm in 1962 as it was later to become. It was strong enough, however, to motivate his delineation of the center ("City of Harlem"), character ("Street Protest"), and cuisine ("Soul Food") of a sui generis terrain. Moreover, it was sufficiently unequivocal to bring forth revised definitions of art and the function of the artist. The premise of "The Myth of a Negro Literature" is that black American writers prior to the 1960s produced nothing but mediocre works. Their creative shortcomings, according to Baraka, resulted from their deserting the emotional references of their own culture in order to imitate the norms of white middle-class life and art in America. By contrast, "Negro music . . . because it drew its strengths and beauties out of the depth of the black man's soul and because to a large extent its traditions could be carried on by the lowest classes of Negroes, has been able to survive the constant and willful dilutions of the black middle class" (*Home,* p. 106). Clearly, Baraka realizes the traps that the English language and the general public discourse about black America have presented for the black spokesman. He insists, therefore, that only the music of black America has provided an adequate source of expression for black culture as a whole. Given the issues raised by Douglass's and Washington's autobiographical acts, one can see how a black nationalist prospect such as Baraka's might set great store by an abstract art form such as music. Baldwin, however, provided a caution about black music that one cannot ignore; he speaks of the covering sentimentality of the music that allows whites to enjoy it without ever hearing its harsher notes. The notion of culturally unique meanings in black literary texts (which has been insisted upon up to now) brings works like Douglass's *Narrative* or Wheatley's "To the University of Cambridge, in New England" within a framework similar to the one Baldwin notes for black music: the surface sentiments of black literary texts can obscure their more substantive meanings for the unwary observer. Considering Baraka's nationalist and anti-middle-class orientation, however, it is not surprising that he suggests that black writers in the future should emulate such culturally distinctive forms as jazz and blues, which have their origins in black folk life. What is particularly striking from the author who saw the poem as "a turning away" is the following conception of "high art":

> High art, first of all, must reflect the experiences of the human being, the emotional predicament of man, as he exists, in the

> defined world of his being.... High art, and by this I mean any art that would attempt to describe or characterize some portion of the profound meaningfulness of human life with any finality or truth, cannot be based on the superficialities of human existence. It must issue from real categories of human activity, *truthful* accounts of human life, and not fancied accounts of the attainment of cultural privilege by some willingly preposterous apologist for one social "order" or another. [*Home*, p. 109]

Baraka concludes that black American literature has never fulfilled the positive requirements set forth in this passage because its writers have always accepted a distorted conception of history rendered by white American liberals. He goes on to assert that Western and American history, for the black man, began with the slave trade (*Home*, p. 111). Only a close attention to the "emotional history of the black man in this country," which differs from that of the dominant group, enables a black writer to provide works of cultural relevance (*Home*, p. 112). If the black writer adopts the prevailing white bourgeoisie's conception of reality, he will not find himself reflected in it at all because white America does not admit that a unique black man—one unaccounted for by white social codes—exists (*Home*, p. 113). For a black writer to adopt such a perspective is for him to write "after the fact" (*Home*, p. 112), i.e., to take up a life devoid of cultural significance.

Baraka's extensions of the foregoing propositions include a view of the virtues in segregation. Since blacks have never been able to cross the no-man's-land that exists between black and white in America, they have retained a specificity of cultural reference that gives "logic and beauty" to their music (*Home*, p. 114). This fact, if acknowledged by black writers, promises an important place in the world for black literature:

> At this point when the whole of Western society might go up in flames, the Negro remains an integral part of that society, but continually outside it, a figure like Melville's Bartleby. He is an American, capable of identifying emotionally with the fantastic cultural ingredients of this society, but he is also, forever, outside that culture, an invisible strength within it,

> an observer. If there is ever a Negro literature, it must disengage itself from the weak, heinous elements of the culture that spawned it, and use its very existence as evidence of a more profound America. [*Home,* pp. 114–15]

Although the quotation moves in Western and American terms, it foreshadows Baraka's complete departure from the West. Black literature's "disengagement" from the West, that is to say, can scarcely occur without a withdrawal from the Western arena by the black writer. The vision of a West in flames foreshadows Baraka's own strategy of combining his decision to leave the arena with dire projections of an American apocalypse.

By 1962, Baraka's careful, reflective, insightful prefigurations were in order. It should have come as no surprise in 1964, then, to see an essay from his pen entitled, "Last Day of the American Empire (Including Some Instructions for Black People)." The essay concludes: "The hope is that young blacks will remember all of their lives what they are seeing, what they are witness to just by being alive and black in America, and that eventually they will use this knowledge sicentifically, and erupt like Mt. Vesuvius to crush in hot lava these willful maniacs who call themselves white Americans" (*Home,* p. 209). The artistic form that will capture a coming Armageddon, says Baraka, is "the Revolutionary Theatre": "The Revolutionary Theatre must teach them [white men] their deaths. It must crack their faces open to the mad cries of the poor. It must teach them about silence and the truths lodged there. It must kill any God anyone names except Common Sense. The Revolutionary Theatre should flush the fags and murders out of Lincoln's face" (*Home,* p. 211). It must "show the missionaries and wiggly Liberals dying under blasts of concrete. For sound effects, wild screams of joy, from all the peoples of the world" (*Home,* p. 211).

Adopting the perspective of the victim, the revolutionary theater moves toward change. It is a social art, "where real things can be said about a real world" (*Home,* p. 212). At the point of imagination, it is an almost mystical enterprise:

"Imagination (Image) is all possibility, because from the image, the initial circumscribed energy, any use (idea) is possible. And so begins that image's use in the world. Possibility is what moves us" (*Home,* p. 213). The playwright, therefore, not only assaults whatever stands in the way of man's freedom, but also provides the necessary images for a transformation of the world. The forceful and aggressive manner in which he portrays society's victims will cause them to rush from the theater and cleanse the universe. When there are no more victims, other heroes will appear—revolutionary leaders like Denmark Vesey and Crazy Horse. The stage will then be set for the emergence of the "new man" (*Home,* pp. 214–15). Hence the power of the artistic image properly employed is the power to create a new world.

This conceptualization of the power of the verbal structure, as we have seen in Douglass and other writers treated up to now, is not new to black writing. What is original with Baraka is the direction in which he wishes to turn the force of the word. The intention of the speech act is murder, to eliminate the larger white world altogether. There is no thought of moving into white culture by "doing things with words"; the aim is rather to bring into existence an autonomous and more humane black world. Other black writers, such as Martin Delany and W. E. B. Du Bois (as we shall see later), had anticipated Baraka in assuming this position, but none had taken it up with his competence and clarity.

Baraka calls the writings in *Home* "social essays," and their progression from "Cuba Libre" to "The Revolutionary Theatre" does reflect the tendency (discussed earlier) of black people in America to raise their arms with ever-increasing militancy as the sixties progressed. Mirroring the "social" mood of the decade, Baraka moved from the bohemian mask of *Preface* to the guise of a writer bringing down the roof-beams of an unjust world. His early concern with Western values and literature declined as he adopted the stance of a rebellious writer in harmony with the emotional references of his own culture. African blues still might not have recognized him, but neither did the radical chic denizens of Bohemia or the casual liberals of the academy.

Two 1964 plays, *Dutchman* and *The Slave*,[4] serve to explain. Clay, the black protagonist of *Dutchman*, delivers a long, bitter tirade after he and Lula (the play's white lead) have engaged in a series of clever word games. Like the American liberals whom Baraka damns so unequivocally, Lula is a "wiggly" liar trapped by her own fantasies. She is also a bohemian like the one described in "American Sexual Reference: Black Male": "for the white woman it [being a liberated artist or entertainer] means at one point, that she has more liberal opinions, or at least likes to bask in the gorgeousness of being hip, or, sophisticated, outcast. There is a whole social grouping of white women who are body-missionaries" (*Home*, p. 223). Unable to avoid the myths fostered by a "Liberal/Missionary syndrome" and by Bohemia, Clay and Lula have no choice but to pursue their deadly verbal exchange. But the woman pushes too far—to that place where Clay, who has been shedding the bonds of his Western clothing throughout the play, must retaliate in vicious terms. In essence, he tells Lula that all blacks hate all whites, that the proof of this is found in black art, and that once blacks cease to sublimate their anger, they will rise up and murder their white oppressors. The three-piece-suit-wearing black intellectual, who was once fond of Baudelaire and other white ideas, becomes a poet screaming his madness into the face of the white world. His speech is one act in the revolutionary theater. And his role as victim is dramatically highlighted when he moves to retrieve his belongings from the seat where Lula sits. She stabs him to death.

Though Clay is usually seen as the hero of *Dutchman*, I think the play's real subject is Lula. Certainly her final action drives home the accuracy of Baraka's 1962 claim that "if, right this minute, I were, in some strange fit of irrationality, to declare that 'I am a free man and have the right of complete self-determination,' chances are that I would be dead or in jail by nightfall" (*Home*, p. 79). The "irrational" black man who asserts his liberation and projects the destruction of America has no place in Lula's scheme of existence—except the cemetery, or prison. Yet he is real, and Baraka goes on to picture him in clearer outline in *The Slave*.

Walker Vessels is the black idealist caught in the throes of reconciling his subjective notions of a more attractive world with the mayhem required to translate his vision into objective reality. The only thing Walker is certain of is that the white liberal is the major obstacle to his goal. In other words, he is not as convinced of the undeniable rightness of his own ideas as he is of the undeniable wrongness of his adversary's. One of his exchanges with his white former college professor, Bradford Easley, clarifies this:

> EASLEY You're so wrong about everything.... Do you think Negroes are better people than whites... that they can govern a society *better* than whites?... So the have-not peoples become the haves. Even so, will that change the essential functions of the world? Will there be more love or beauty in the world... more knowledge... because of this?
> WALKER Probably. Probably there will be more... if more people have a chance to understand what it is. But that's not even the point. It comes down to baser human endeavor than any social-political thinking. What does it matter if there's more love or beauty?... The point is that you had your chance, darling, now these other folks have theirs.
>
> [*Slave*, p. 73]

Easley says in response: "God, what an ugly idea." And Walker insists that it is exactly the kind of brusque, defensive insularity signaled by Easley's response that ensures the world's ugliness. For the professor is, finally, a man who feels that evil should not be confronted but left to die of its own accord. No, says Walker, "right is in the act! And the act itself has some place in the world... it makes some place for itself":

> WALKER Yeah, well, I know I thought then that none of you could write any poetry either. I knew that you had moved too far away from the actual meanings of life... into some lifeless cocoon of pretended intellectual and emotional achievement, to really be able to see the world again. What was Rino writing before he got killed. Tired elliptical little descriptions of what he could see out the window.
>
> [*Slave*, pp. 75–76]

The dialogue ends when Walker shoots Easley, and the house comes crashing down under the blasts of the liberation army. The idealistic artist turned revolutionary is a startling figure for Easley. And though Walker's propensities for the old days—seen in his attempts to baffle the professor with quotations from Yeats and his concern for his white former wife (Grace)—show through, *The Slave* ends on the last day of the American liberal-intellectual empire.

While both *Dutchman* and *The Slave* were first staged downtown, the progress of the artist revealed by the plays had impelled Baraka uptown—to Harlem. "I Don't Love You," a poem from *Target Study,* describes this move in powerful terms:

> Whatever you've given me, whiteface glass
> to look through, to find another there, another
> what motherfucker? another bread tree mad at its
> sacredness, and the law of some dingaling god, cold
> as ice cucumbers, for the shouters and the wigglers,
> and what was the world to the words of slick nigger
> fathers, too depressed to explain why they could not
> appear to be men.
> The bread fool. The don'ts of this white hell. The
> crashed eyes
> of dead friends, standing at the bar, eyes focused on
> actual ugliness.
> I don't love you. Who is to say what that will mean.
> I don't love you, expressed the train, moves and uptown
> days later we look up and breathe much easier
> I don't love you.[5]

The certainty that rings through the poem was purchased at agonizing cost, as Baraka's 1964 volume of poetry, *The Dead Lecturer,* illustrates. The title is appropriate, since so many of the individual poems are concerned with the poet's loss of feeling, the tortures brought on by his severance from an old life. He speaks, for example, of "the perversity / of separation, isolation, / after so many years of trying to enter their kingdoms . . ."[6] And the source of human contact seen in *Preface*—the fingers—is drawn as follows: "(Inside his books, his fingers. They / are withered yellow flowers and were never / beautiful)" (*Dead Lecturer,* p. 15). The waters, which are viewed as signs of a world containing at least the possibility of love in the earlier work, have been transmuted:

> (Love twists
> the young man. Having seen it
> only once. He expected it
> to be, as the orange flower
> leather of the poet's book.
> He expected
> less hurt, a lyric. And not
> the slow effortless pain
> as a new dripping sun pushes
> up out of our river.)
>   And
> having seen it, refuses
> to inhale. "It was a
> green mist, seemed
> to lift and choke
> the town."
>
> [*Dead Lecturer,* p. 17]

The attractive existence of his bohemian days has disappeared: "———They have passed / and gone / whom you thot your lovers" (*Dead Lecturer,* p. 31). Finally the poet can describe himself only as "inside someone who hates me" (*Dead Lecturer,* p. 15), and as one who is:

> . . . deaf and blind and lost and will not again sing
> your quiet verse. I have lost
> even the act of poetry, and writhe now for cool
> horizonless dawn.
>
> [*Dead Lecturer,* p. 47]

The political poems in *The Dead Lecturer* explore some of the reasons for this painful condition. In "A Contract. (For the Destruction and Rebuilding of Paterson)," "A Poem for Neutrals," "A Poem for Democrats," and "The Politics of Rich Painters," Baraka attacks the corruption of art and life that has resulted from the West's domination of the world. To live the chic bohemian life of a "neutral" artist in the face of such disaster is a betrayal of humanity. Lines from "Green Lantern's Solo" reflect both the motives for the poet's move to a separate, black life in Harlem and the immediate anguish that accompanied it:

> ... What man unremoved from his meat's source can
> continue to believe totally in himself? Or on the
> littered sidewalks of his personal
> history, can continue to believe in his own dignity
> or intelligence.
> Except the totally ignorant
> who are our leaders.
>   Except the completely devious
>   Who are our lovers.
>
> [*Dead Lecturer*, pp. 68–69]

The pressing need to touch his "meat's source" forced Baraka to step beyond the loves and lovers of the past; they were adjuncts to what he came to see as a sick world. Yet the uncertainty of his transition stands out in the concluding lines of *The Dead Lecturer:*

> When they say, "It is Roi
> who is dead?" I wonder
> who will they mean?

Baraka was part of a group of black artists who established the Harlem Black Arts Repertory Theatre School, an enterprise devoted to ideas and ideals set forth most effectively in *Home*. Street theater, creative writing workshops, poetry readings, lectures, exhibitions, and other events designed to heighten the consciousness of a black urban community were included in the organization's activities. Baraka asserted that "Black Art" had now been officially ushered into the world and securely housed. But he also knew it had come on the winds of a spiraling nationalism. His 1965 essays in *Home* treat "The Legacy of Malcolm X, and the Coming of the Black Nation" as corollaries to an even further revised definition of the artist. Malcolm is described as a man who "made the consideration of Nationalist ideas significant and powerful in our day" (*Home*, p. 241), who

> wanted to give the Nationalist Consciousness its political embodiment, and send it out to influence the newly forming third world, in which this consciousness was to be included. The concept of Blackness, the concept of the National Consciousness, the proposal of a political (and diplomatic) form

> for this aggregate of Black spirit, these are the things given to us by Garvey, through Elijah Muhammed and finally given motion into still another area of Black response by Malcolm X. [*Home,* p. 243]

Three concepts merge under this general conception of nationalism: race, nation, and culture. The last is seen as the most salient since it constitutes an agency of consciousness: "What a culture produces, and refers to, is an image—a picture of a process, since it is a form of a process: movement seen. The changing of images, of references, is the Black Man's way back to the racial integrity of the captured African, which is where we must take ourselves, in feeling, to be truly the warriors we propose to be" (*Home,* p. 247). Having emphasized once again the importance of the cultural image, Baraka lays out the following dictates for the black artist: "The Black Artist's role in America is to aid the destruction of America as we know it. . . . The Black Artist must draw out of his soul the correct image of the world. He must use this image to bond his brothers and sisters together in common understanding of the nature of the world (and the nature of America) and the nature of the human soul" (*Home,* p. 252).

Both the idea of culture and the specification of the artist's function are rooted in what might be called a black sense of manifest destiny. Baraka says: "God is man realized. The Black man must realize himself as Black. And idealize and aspire to that" (*Home,* p. 248). The ultimate goal is black humanism. But if the nation can evolve only through a cultural consciousness that flows from the soul of the artist, it seems that Baraka is suggesting a conflation of God and the black artist. In other words, the writer is a man like all other men, but one who is more completely realized, as God. He becomes, therefore, the leader in a divinely inspired crusade for black cultural nationalism. The difference between Baraka's formulation and Baldwin's aesthetics is that Baraka's is fiercely social. It calls for real change in the actual world.

Baraka's revised view led him in at least two clear social directions, yielding first the agitprop dramas of *Four Black Revolutionary Plays* and *Jello.* With the exception of *A Black*

Mass these works conform closely to the requirements for a "Revolutionary Theatre." In *Experimental Death Unit #1, Great Goodness of Life,* and *Madheart,* black victims are parodied, castigated, or shown in the throes of horrible deaths. Duff and Loco, the white characters of *Experimental Death Unit #1,* are appropriately crushed by the bullets of a black liberation army—not before they have been rendered patently grotesque by their dialogue and actions, however. *A Black Mass* stands out from the company because its tone and language are elevated to match a sophisticated ideational framework. The conflict between Jacoub and his fellow "magicians" is one between the restless, empirical inventor and the mystical artist who feels his oneness with all things. Finally, Jacoub creates both time and a hideous white beast who adores it under the following sanction: "Let us be fools. For creation is its own end."[7] *A Black Mass* employs the demonology of the Nation of Islam, but in Baraka's hands the drama's story takes on the character of a lyrical, mythopoeic exchange designed to guide the energies of the new Black Arts Movement. The play is dedicated to "the brothers and sisters of The Black Arts." *Jello,* by comparison, is a broad farce designed to show the traditional house servant (in this case, Rochester of the Jack Benny establishment) transforming himself into a revolutionary.

The other direction pursued by Baraka in the years immediately following the establishment of the Black Arts Repertory Theatre School was an art of specific recall. Lines from *The Dead Lecturer* project both the style and substance of this enterprise:

> . . . Nothing is ever finished. Nothing past. Each
> act of my life, with me now, till death. Themselves,
> the reasons for it. They are stones, in my mouth
> and ears. Whole forests on my shoulders.
>
> [*Dead Lecturer,* p. 36]

> What comes, closest, is
> closest. Moving, there
> is a wreck of spirit,
> a heap of broken feeling. What

was only love
or in those cold rooms,
opinion. Still, it made
color. And filled me
as no one will. As, even
I cannot fill
myself.

[*Dead Lecturer*, p. 54]

In a sense, Baraka—like William Carlos Williams, whose work played a role in the black writer's early development—is a regional author molding the details of a particular New Jersey landscape into an endless array of meanings. A number of short stories in *Tales* and the moving autobiographical narration of *The System of Dante's Hell* are products of an artist who knew life was shaped by things as simple as "a green truck." There is a telling personal significance in Walker Vessel's statement that "the aesthete came long after all the things that really formed me" (*Slave*, p. 75).

Baraka uses the cryptic language of the aesthete, however, to sketch those exact portrayals of his school experiences in Newark ("Uncle Tom's Cabin: Alternative Ending," "The Largest Ocean in the World") and his term in the United States Air Force ("Salute") that appear in *Tales*. In these stories, the painful events of his past are rehearsed, mulled over, until they yield their precise character. If one seeks a definition of the process, it might be Ellison's delineation of the blues: "an impulse to keep the painful details and episodes of a brutal experience alive in one's aching consciousness, to finger its jagged grain, and to transcend it, not by the consolation of philosophy but by squeezing from it a near-tragic, near-comic lyricism. As a form, the blues is an autobiographical chronicle of personal catastrophe expressed lyrically" (*Shadow and Act*, p. 90). This might serve as a description of the ending of "Salute," in which Baraka details his coming into literature and the fanciful world into which this carried him. Jolted from his reverie by a lieutenant who says, "Don't you know you're supposed to salute officers?" Baraka describes his reaction:

> When the focus returned. (Mine) I don't know what that means. Focus, returned . . . that 's not precise enough. Uh . . . I meant, when I could finally say something to this guy . . . I didin't have anything to say. But I knew that in the first place. I said, "Yes sir, I know all about it." No, I didn't say any such shit as that. I said, "Well, if the airplanes blow up, Chinese with huge habits will drop out of the sky, riding motorized niggers," You know I didn't say that. But I said something, you know, the kind of shit you'd say, you know.[8]

The ending of "Salute" is one of the clearer illustrations of Baraka's technique. At times, his references are so intensely personal that it is almost impossible for the reader to grasp the object or event represented. At such moments, the narrator is a lonely musician riffing to himself, as in a number of instances in *The System of Dante's Hell*. But on the whole, that novel offers an exciting and coherent account of the development of a black man who was born into the world "pointed in the right direction" and slowly moved away from the nurturing sights and smells of his birthplace into a sterile region of middle-class pretense and denial. The road traveled is described by *System* as one leading outward from the childhood gang (the "Secret Seven") to places of music and "hip" bell-bottom suits like those portrayed in the chapter "The Christians." College and the air force push the narrator even closer to that final, heretical denial that comprises the last chapter of the work: "Fire burns around the tombs. Closed from the earth. A despair came down. Alien grace. Lost to myself, I'd come back. To that ugliness sat inside me waiting. And the mere sky greying could do it."[9] Having almost surrendered to the black South represented by the "bottom" in Shreveport, Louisiana, he draws back. He turns inward, and after a fight with three inhabitants of the bottom, in which he is leveled, he somehow manages to return to the air force base. He awakens three days later with the feeling that his entire experience among the blacks transpired in a cave where he sat reading. The room of *Preface* and Plato's cave merge as signs of the solipsistic artist.

But there is a certain tension in the concluding lines; the author is aware of his role as a blues artist: "I sat reading from a book aloud and they [black people] danced to my reading" (*System*, p. 152). The redemptive value of Baraka's regional, personal art is perhaps captured by this image. It is described in more lyrical terms in lines from "Leadbelly Gives an Autograph":

> The possibilities of music. First
> that it does exist. And that we do,
> in that scripture of rhythms. The earth,
> I mean the soil, as melody. The fit you need,
> the throes. To pick it up and cut
> away what does not singularly express.
>
> [*Black Magic*, p. 25]

Seeking black music as his model, Baraka hoped to avoid the subtle incarcerations entailed by language. His autobiographical recall is less exposition than lyric, and the journey depicted is a harrowing descent into the hell of a self misshaped by Western values. The narrator is not searching for a way to corral the supposed benefits of the white world. Instead, he is attempting to push language to its highest range in order to exorcize the demons who have misrouted his life. Intensity is the norm. He strains against "painful details" in a quest for the wholeness of the black self. The irony is his choice of a framework. The question, "What are influences?" posed in *Preface*, poses itself once more. Surely Dante and the specific world of literacy an acquaintance with the medieval Italian author implies were salient influences for Baraka. *System* may be the narrator's music, but like Tolson's *Libretto* it requires a sophisticated listener. In this sense the work is a higher-order attenuation of such developmental accounts as Vassa's and Douglass's. But there is yet an additional irony to be noted. Baraka, unlike either of his predecessors, had achieved a kind of hyperliteracy. Although he was aware of the pitfalls involved, he dared to appropriate the name and instrumentalities of one of the most brilliant Western poets, and he turned both to his own unique ends. Rather than the rudimentary seizing of the word, his autobiographical act is a declaration of the black literary artist—with a capital "A."

The poems of *Black Art,* which were written in 1965 and 1966, the essays of *Raise Race Rays Raze* (1971), and the verse of *Spirit Reach* (1972) are extensions of Baraka's previously articulated positions. They harmonize disparate tendencies in his work of the mid-decade. The preoccupation with an art of specific recall, for example, and revolutionary nationalism combine in the writer's projection of Newark as the black urban community that will serve as a model for the new world of black humanism.

In "Newark—Before Black Men Conquered," he starts by analyzing his birthplace as an example of domestic colonialism: "There is a clearer feeling in Newark, than any other city I have ever been in, of Colonialism. Newark is *a colony.* A bankrupt ugly colony, in the classic term, where white people make their money to take away with them."[10] Blacks who inhabit Newark, therefore, are (perforce) separate. They are not susceptible to American definitions (*Raise Race,* pp. 78–79). Having continually served as chattel, they must now rise and seize power: "These cities: Newark, Gary, Washington, Detroit, Richmond, Harlem, Oakland, East St. Louis, Bedford-Stuyvesant, etc. any large concentration of Black people . . . almost always disunified, but these are our kingdoms, and this is where we must first rule . . . . The cities must be Black ruled or they will not be ruled at all!" (*Raise Race,* p. 79).

The extension of earlier definitions occurs in terms of black manifest destiny. In "A School Prayer," a poem from *Black Art,* the poet says:

> The eye sees. The I. The self. Which passes out and
> into the wind. We are so beautiful we talk at the same
> time and our breathing is harnessed to divinity.
>
> [*Black Magic,* p. 121]

In "The Spell," he continues:

> . . . The eyes of God-our on us
> in us. The Spell. We are wisdom, reaching for itself.
> We are
> totals, watch us, watch through yourself, and become
> the whole

> universe at once so beautiful you will become, without having moved, or gone through a "change," except to be moving with
> the world,
> at that incredible speed, with all the genius of a tree.
>
> [*Black Magic*, p. 147]

The same theme appears in "The Calling Together":

> Energies exploding
> Black World Renewed
> Sparks! Stars! Eyes!
> Huge Holocausts of Heaven
> Burning down the white man's world
> Holy ashes!!!
> Let the rains melt them into rivers.
> And the new people naked bathe themselves
> And look upon the life to come as the heaven
> we
> seek
>
> [*Black Magic*, p. 174]

"Black People: This Is Our Destiny," with its insistence that the rhythms of the "holy black man" are in harmony with those of the universe, offers a final example:

> . . . vibration holy nuance beating against
> itself, a rhythm a playing reunderstood now by one of the
> 1st race
> the primitives the first men who evolve again to civilize
> the
> world
>
> [*Black Magic*, p. 199]

The consciousness needed to effect this destiny comes from within:

> . . .We are no thing, we are every space
> of living. We are flying without airplanes, cooking
> without stoves. Touch God and know him, look into
> your screaming brain. In those chambers the real way lurks
> in the shadow of your meaningless desires. The
> real breath of where we moved toward, the perfection
> of space.
>
> [*Black Magic*, p. 209]

And the black poet as the man through whom the divine sanctions for new order flow is seen in "All in the Street":

> . . . Listen to the creator
> speak in me now. Listen, these words
> are part of God's thing. I am a
> vessel, a black priest interpreting
> the present & future for my people
> Olorun—Allah speaks in and
> thru me now . . . He begs me to
> pray for you—as I am doing—He
> bids me have you submit to
> the energy.[11]

By the beginning of the seventies, Baraka could say:

> There is no such thing as art and politics, there is only life, and its many registrations. If the artist is the raised consciousness then all he touches, all that impinges on his consciousness must be raised. We must be the will of the race toward evolution . . . THE LARGEST WORK OF ART IS THE WORLD ITSELF. The potential is unlimited. [*Raise Race*, p. 129]

His voice became political, saying: "WE MUST BE IN THE REAL WORLD. WE MUST BE ACTUAL DOERS" (*Raise Race*, p. 101). In March of 1972, he was a forceful spokesman at the National Black Political Convention, which met in Gary, Indiana, to discuss pragmatic ways to improve the condition of blacks in America. Since that time, he has moved away from his nationalist stance to endorse what he calls "Marxism-Leninism-Mao-Tse-Tung-Thought." Though Marxism and nationalism are incompatible at many levels, Baraka's ideals for the "raised" cultural consciousness and his increasing political involvement in the "real world" make scientific socialism one feasible outgrowth of his activities. In *Raise Race Rays Raze* he says "Do not talk of Marx or Lenin or Trotsky when you speak of political thinkers" (p. 95). But a reading of his canon reveals enough concern for the economics of colonialism and the politics of national liberation in the Third World to provide an explanation for his shift to a Marxist frame of reference. His contact with Amilcar Cabral and other African socialist thinkers surely heightened his conviction that the "mystical or cult nationalism which is not about political struggle" is a less effective strategy than theoretical analyses which begin with the material base of society.[12] Moreover, a theological stance for the leader possessing a heightened consciousness has not been alien to the actual manifestations of Marxism-Leninism or Maoist thought in our day. One of the most significant aspects of this change of loyalities is that it reflects black America's growing disenchantment with a strict cultural nationalism. Baraka's is but one of the many revised or altered strategies adopted by blacks in the lean, quiet years since Watergate. Nonetheless, one has the feeling that his current posture augurs war no less surely than his position of a few years back: "we [advocates for a new communist party] represent working people and oppressed nationalities who when they find out what has to be done, that a revolution is what is needed, will sweep all slow babblers and jivers aside and destroy all forms of oppression and exploitation by means of the armed seizure of state power."[13] The man who was "thinking of a dance" at the beginning of the sixties has found his music:

> BANZAI!! BANZAI!! BANZAI!! BANZAI!! BANZAI!!
> came running out of the drugstore with
> an electric alarm clock, and then dropped the motherfucker
> and broke it. Go get something else. Take everything
>   in there.
> Look in the cash register. TAKE THE MONEY. TAKE THE MONEY.
>   YEH.
> TAKE IT ALL. YOU DON'T HAVE TO CLOSE THE DRAWER. COME ON
>   MAN, I SAW
> A TAPE RECORDER BACK THERE.
>   These are the words of lovers.
>   Of dancers, of dynamite singers
>   These are songs if you have the
>   music
>
> [*Black Magic*, p. 104]

Baraka must occupy an extensive space in any account of black American literature during the sixties. He both anticipated and assumed most of the major positions that characterized black writers of the decade. The signal aspect of his development is his attempt to construct and articulate a new conception of black America. Contrary to the country's accepted notion, he states that the American and his history, as conceived by a white liberal intellectual establishment, are not ideal entities standing at the acme of human achievement. The notion that they are, he insists, is rooted in a history of oppression and destruction. It is a sophisticated version of all Western rationalizations designed to mollify guilt. In successive works, Baraka brings convincing evidence and enormous passion to the justification of his position. He concludes that black Americans have absolutely no cause to accept white America's fundamental notion or to elaborate a course of action that will bring their own condition into harmony with it. Instead, blacks must look before and after and work to create a humane way of life overseen by men and women who possess a knowledge of their culture and understand its abiding distinctiveness from the West's. The black nation is seen as the agency of an evolutionary process in which blacks will realize themselves as the "new people" of the earth. With his advocacy of Marxism-Leninism-Mao-Tse-Tung-Thought in the seventies, the composition of Baraka's "new" world has become more diverse (an international working class), but the unified black nation is still an important prerequisite. The brilliantly projected conception of black as a country—a separate and progressive nation with values antithetical to those of white America—stands in marked contrast to the ideas set forth by Baldwin, Wright, Ellison, and others in the fifties.

During the earlier decade, black writers did suggest that their roles might be different from those of white authors. And they often looked to the Third World. They were patently aware that redefinitions were in order. But they maintained always a reserved and, in some cases, a passionate attachment to the West. Ellison and Wright knew the shortcomings of Europe and America, yet both accentuated what they saw as redeeming qualities of Western history. Baldwin, working in a similar vein, proposed the Western artistic heritage as a means of achieving the mysteries of the self. And many black authors who gathered to discuss their function spoke in solemn tones of the future day when the great Western promise of equality would be fulfilled. Few assumed a truly nationalistic voice. Politics were forbidden at the Sorbonne, and in New York the most radical strategy to emerge was exile—in Africa, or in an African sensibility defined by Negritude. While foreshadowings of the revolt to come were apparent in the fifties, black writing during the decade remained fundamentally Western in outlook and tone. No black writer in full possession of his senses wanted to be just like his white predecessors and contemporaries, but many insisted, sometimes vigorously, that their past, present, and future had to be comprehended in Western terms.

Their insistence does not, I think, constitute irony, paradox, or treachery. It simply illustrates (in a very Barakan way) that the American mechanisms designed either to placate the dispossessed or to win them to a belief in an "apprenticeship for freedom" are always operative. Their prototypes can be seen in the laws, bills, statutes, and assurances mentioned in conjunction with Douglass. They are always presented in the form of invitations to join a company of white dreamers. Moreover, there was a slight suspension during the fifties of the extreme violence and repression that blacks had come to regard as daily fare since the end of the nineteenth century; a mild breathing space opened for an instant. The real irony lies in the fact that the black masses took what America intended as a momentary gesture—*Brown* v. *Board of Education*—as a sanction for their unprecedented surge forward. Suddenly there were hundreds of thousands of blacks demanding "Freedom Now!" When the media reported in lurid detail the bitterness and intensity of this movement, it must have shocked older black writers to discover that theirs was a passionate people indeed. The existence of a mass black audience, with its mind set on something quite different from the traditional forms of high art, must have been even more surprising.

The confrontations that came in the wake of the accelerating black liberation struggle have been sketched above.

Their consequences were severe enough to convince some of the most ardent black disciples that the West could not survive the test at hand. In the early years of the sixties, therefore, talk of "black Western man" rapidly subsided. It was replaced by prophecies of the last days of the American empire, and the newly emergent black audience was a prime consideration. These addresses were avowedly political and militantly activist in orientation. A new identity, a new nation, seemed possible because black people, in ever-increasing number, were demanding both. In sum, black writers of the fifties were not certain they had a country. They worked, perhaps too often, in a world of abstractions that included not only their most esteemed values, but also their hypothetical, or implied, Western audience. In the sixties and seventies, on the other hand, black spokesmen were convinced that their real audience, like the nation to come, was black, and their values and canons were designed to accord with this conviction.

The strength of this conviction, moreover, was sufficient to bring about significant shifts in the work of several black writers from earlier generations. Gwendolyn Brooks, winner of the Pulitzer Prize for poetry in 1950, offers an example. In the mid-sixties, Brooks was indisputably the most celebrated living black American poet. She had been lauded by the Midwestern Writer's Conference, the John Simon Guggenheim Memorial Foundation, and countless other agencies of American arts and letters. Her dazzling word-magic had secured the favor of white publishers and reviewers alike. She describes herself in *Report from Part One* as an "old girl"—one from the very select group of black writers who had made their way in the white literary establishment. She goes on, however, to detail her experiences at the 1967 Fisk University Writers' Conference:

> Coming from white white white South Dakota State College I arrived in Nashville, Tennessee, to give one more "reading." But blood-boiling surprise was in store for me. First, I was aware of a general energy, an electricity, in look, walk, speech, gesture of the young blackness I saw all about me. I had been "loved" at South Dakota State College. Here, I was

> coldly respected.... Imamu Amiri Baraka, then "LeRoi Jones," was expected. He arrived in the middle of my own offering, and when I called attention to his presence there was jubilee in Jubilee Hall.... All that day and night... an almost hysterical Gwendolyn B. walked about in amazement, listening, looking, learning. *What was going on!*[14]

Her bafflement soon became the certainty that "there is indeed a new black today. He is different from any the world has known" (*Report,* p. 85). She also discovered that the artists in the group were directing their energies to the creation of a new nation and their voices to an audience radically different from any she had ever conceived of. Discussing her interaction with black writers in Chicago, she says:

> Well, right around the corner is a tavern, and one Sunday afternoon, some of the poets decided to go in there and read poetry. I went with them. One of them went to the front of the tavern and said, "Say folks, we're going to lay some poetry on you."... The poets started reading, and before we knew it, people had turned around on their bar stools, with their drinks behind them, and were listening. Then they applauded. [*Report,* p. 152]

Jolted from what she calls "a sweet ignorance," Brooks cast her lot with the new generation. Conducting poetry workshops in Chicago's South Side black community, meeting with developing writers in her home, and moving among black people intent on their own nation she came to a new resolve: "My aim, in my next future, is to write poems that will somehow successfully "call" (see Imamu Baraka's "SOS") all black people: black people in taverns, black people in alleys, black people in gutters, schools, offices, factories, prisons, the consulate; I wish to reach black people in pulpits, black people in mines, on farms, on thrones" (*Report,* p. 183).

Since 1967, Brooks has indeed reached out to a black audience. Her early poem "Negro Hero," written "to suggest Dorie Miller," a black ship's steward who rushed on deck to man the guns during an enemy attack in World War II, begins:

> I had to kick their law into their teeth in order to save them.
> However I have heard that sometimes you have to deal
> Devilishly with drowning men in order to swim them to shore.[15]

And her long poem of the same period, "The Anniad," contains the following wry reflection on its heroine:

> Think of thaumaturgic lass
> Looking in her looking-glass
> At the unembroidered brown;
> Printing bastard roses there;
> Then emotionally aware
> Of the black and boisterous hair
> Taming all that anger down.[16]

The difference between the foregoing and Brooks's more recent work is illustrated by a figure like Way-out Morgan of *In the Mecca:*

> Way-out Morgan is collecting guns
> in a tiny fourth-floor room.
> He is not hungry, ever, though sinfully lean.
> He flourishes, ever, on porridge or pat of bean
> pudding or wiener soup—fills fearsomely
> on visions of Death-to-the-Hoardes-of-the-White-Men!
> Death!
> (This is the Maxim painted in big black
> above a bed bought at a Champlain rummage sale.)[17]

Just as Way-out Morgan—for all his rummage-sale furniture and too-intense revolutionary display—is a quantum leap from the Negro hero, so Mary Ann of "The Blackstone Rangers" is light-years away from the sensitive and troubled Annie Allen: "Mary is / a rose in a whisky glass" (*Mecca,* p. 47).

The ironies that Brooks directed at supercilious whites and the detached, subtle amusement with which she approached some black subjects in earlier work[18] are absent in poems like "Malcolm X," "Medgar Evers," and "The Second Sermon on the Warpland." Her more recent poetry stands in fine contrast to products of "the western field." The phrase comes from the first poem of a two-part dedication in *In the Mecca.* Entitled "The Chicago Picasso," it states:

Art hurts. Art urges voyages—
and it is easier to stay at home,
the nice beer ready.
In commonrooms
We belch, or sniff, or scratch.
Are raw.

[*Mecca*, p. 40]

Written to commemorate the unveiling of a Picasso sculpture, the work continues by detailing the demands exercised by those tangible artistic objects before which the individual viewer squirms. While the poet concludes with the romantic notion that art—like a flower in the western field—is its own excuse for being, she goes on to demand more. Her second poem, "The Wall," offers a representation of an entirely different type of art.

A spirit of communality and participation marks the crowd that comes to celebrate the "Wall of Respect," which was painted on a building at 43d and Langley in Chicago to honor black heroes—including Brooks. Instead of the one-to-one (or individualistic) relationship between object and viewer seen in "The Chicago Picasso," the aesthetic experience in "The Wall" is shared by "hundreds of faces, red-brown, brown, black, ivory" (*Mecca*, p. 43). The poet's uncertainty about her role in the group disappears when the members "yield me hot trust, their yea and their Announcement / that they are ready to rile the high-flung ground" (*Mecca*, p. 43). Like a condemned person pardoned an instant before execution, the speaker gladly accepts these reassurances. She and her audience blend as the poem concludes:

An emphasis is paroled.
The old decapitations are revised,
the dispossessions beakless.
And we sing.

[*Mecca*, p. 43]

The "emphasis" which is "paroled" is not only the past life of the speaker. The new energy of the masses is also "paroled," or set in words. The poet, in other words, affirms the ideals of her audience. Past oppression is transcended and transformed as the entire group finds its voice in art.[19]

In *Riot,* a three-part poem written in response to civil disorders in Chicago, Brooks further demonstrates her intention to "call" black people. The poem begins with the demise of John Cabot, a manicured white dilettante. It ends with a resonant black love song. The substance of the middle section is captured by the following lines:

GUARD HERE, GUNS LOADED.
The young men run.
The children in ritual chatter
scatter upon
their Own and old geography.[20]

But like other writers who moved with black America during the sixties, Brooks shows clear signs of disillusionment in her work of the seventies. *Beckonings* begins with "The Boy Died in My Alley," which portrays the speaker as one who has failed in her obligations to her fellows. The work also implies a pervasive and meaningless violence ("the Wild") that seems immemorial in the black community. *Beckonings* closes with the poem "Boys. Black." which urges young blacks to redeem the time. But in this work—unlike in "The Wall"—it is the poet who is the strong force yielding grace:

I tell you
I love you
and I trust you.
Take my Faith.
Make of my Faith an engine.
Make of my Faith
a Black Star. I am Beckoning.[21]

The sentiments are stirring, but they are far from the assured forecasts of *In the Mecca* and *Riot*. "To John Oliver Killens in 1975" addresses the coordinator of the writers' conference from which the poet dates her conversion. It reflects, in disconsolate terms, the sobered mood of black America in the mid-seventies:

John,
look at our mercy, the massiveness that it is not.
Look at our "unity," look at our

"black solidarity,"
Dim, dull and dainty.
Ragged. And we
grow colder; we
grow colder.
See our Tatter-time.

You were a mender.

You were a sealer of tremblings and long trepidations.
And always, with you, the word kindness was not
a jingling thing but an
eye-tenderizer, a
heart-honeyer.

Therefore we turn, John, to you.
Interrupting self-raiding. We pause in our falling.
To ask another question of your daylight.

[*Beckonings*, p. 7]

While one can not say that an "improvement" in Brooks's art resulted from her allegiances of the sixties, one can justifiably infer from her most recent volume that she placed as much faith in the imminence of a new black nation as did her younger contemporaries. *Beckonings* reveals a moving attempt at reassessment, the poet's tribute to those who have maintained the faith ("Five Men against the Theme 'My Name Is Red Hot. Yo Name Ain Doodley Squat'"), and an urgent plea to those who will move our black tomorrows.

Another established writer who underwent a significant transformation during the sixties was James Baldwin. As the founder of a line of black authors who have attacked the protest tradition, Baldwin began his career by assuming the posture discussed in the previous chapter. In 1963, however, he published *Another Country*, an amazingly ambitious novel that attempts a socially responsible critique of American culture as a whole. The first figure encountered in the work is Rufus Scott, a young black musician. Rufus is a down-and-outer, an urban nomad looking for connections. After an engagement at a small club, he finds himself involved with a white southern woman named Leona. The relationship between Rufus and Leona is mythopoeic. Their fierce sexual combats spring directly from the soil of those myths and lies that Baraka delineates in "American Sexual Reference: Black Male." Instead of finding a redemptive union like the one Baldwin urged for black and white Americans in his earlier essays, the couple end by destroying each other. Rufus leaps screaming from the George Washington Bridge. Leona is sent to an asylum. The remainder of the novel traces the implications of the young couple's failure, introducing a desperate and rather unseemly company of souls from Harlem, Paris, and Greenwich Village.

Although Baldwin wrestles with the general dilemmas of artists in American society in *Another Country*—all the major characters are either artists or lovers of artists—his most convincing portrait is that of the raging black "protest" artist, Rufus Scott. True, the writer gives birth to this memorable character only to show him far along the road toward self-destruction. But it is also true that when Baldwin published *Another Country*, he had gone through trials of the spirit that made him cognizant of the real difficulties—if not the impossibility—of being a noninvolved, apolitical black artist in America. Writing in his introduction to *Nobody Knows My Name* about his Parisian self-exile (a condition that had been his since 1948), he says: "It turned out that the question of who I was was not solved because I had removed myself from the social forces which menaced me—anyway, these forces had become interior, and I had dragged them across the ocean with me."[22] As a function of this insight, his artistic concerns become more expansive than he had previously envisioned. Now his true subject becomes "himself *and the world* and it requires every ounce of stamina he can summon to attempt to look on himself and the world as they are" (*Nobody Knows*, p. 12, italics mine).

Upon returning to the United States, Baldwin immediately became active in the civil rights movement. And the stirrings of the struggle led him to the same type of apocalyptic foreshadowings that appear in the work of Baraka. *The Fire Next Time* (1963), a volume containing two essays, predicts the flaming end of the American empire unless those blacks and whites who are morally capable learn to work in harmony. Since 1963, the tone and substance of Baldwin's writings have been profoundly "social." The most disturbing alliance in the life of Leo Proudhammer, a black actor and the protagonist of the novel *Tell Me How Long the Train's Been Gone,* for example, is with Black Christopher, a young militant. Having accepted Christopher as his lover, Leo is not certain what obligations he has to an accelerating black liberation struggle. But he and his lover seem to share a common fate, or destiny. *Tell Me How Long the Train's Been Gone* implies, at least, that the nature of the battle for black freedom will require arming for self-defense. Christopher says, "I know that you love me and you don't want no blood on my hands—dig—but if you don't want me to keep on going under the feet of horses, then I think you got to agree that we need us some guns. Right?" Leo answers, "Yes, I see that."[23] And yet, in the last paragraph of the book, the actor, the black artist, is shown calmly proceeding with his career. He is, in fact, a marvelously successful performer for a general white American audience, still standing in the wings, awaiting his cue. One can not infer, therefore, that the strategies he discusses with Christopher are effected. The author leaves this matter open, as it were, for discussion.

And the irresolution of Baldwin's narrative stance is only modified by two recent works—*No Name in the Street* and *If Beale Street Could Talk. No Name in the Street* is a long expository log of Baldwin's experiences during the latter half of the sixties. The governing conditions of its somber, cynical, at times openly hostile mood are found in the author's reaction to the assassination of Martin Luther King: "Since Martin's death, in Memphis, and that tremendous day [of his funeral] in Atlanta something has altered in me, something has gone away."[24] What has disappeared is Baldwin's belief in the potential for reform of white Americans. The death of King represents a "failure" and "betrayal" that "are in the record book forever, and sum up, and condemn, forever, those descendants of a barbarous Europe who arbitrarily and arrogantly reserve the right to call themselves Americans" (*No Name,* p. 10). The title of Baldwin's essay is extracted from a curse found in the Book of Job: white Americans shall be driven from the world's company and have no name in the street. The writer, however, is not ready to cast off an artistic mantle and attire himself in the drab vestments of revolution. He praises those who have played active roles in civil rights, lauds the Black Panther Party, and even brings the essay toward its close with the following words: "the Western party is over, and the white man's sun has set" (*No Name*, p. 197).

But when he responds to an attack launched on him by a black "revolutionary" (the Eldridge Cleaver of *Soul on Ice*),[25] Baldwin claims that his maligner is a man who attempts to speak for the masses. The artist, says Baldwin, is concerned only with "the person," the individual in society (*No Name*, pp. 171–72). While the revolutionary serves as watchman atop the city wall, the writer pursues his work in a more private quarter. Hence "these two [the artist and the revolutionary] seem doomed to stand forever at an odd and rather uncomfortable angle to each other, and they both stand at a sharp and not always comfortable angle to the people they both, in their different fashions, hope to serve" (*No Name*, p. 172).

One can safely conclude, I think, that Baldwin has not repudiated his belief in the sanctity of the self. Indeed, he says:

> [The] failure of the private life has always had the most devastating effect on American public conduct, and on black-white relations. If Americans were not so terrified of their private selves, they would never have needed to invent and could never have become so dependent on what they still call "the Negro problem" . . . which they invented in order to safeguard their purity. [*No Name*, p. 54]

The affinity between this passage and my previous discussions of acculturation and the nature of the authentic black self in the narrative domain resides in Baldwin's steadfast refusal to surrender himself, or his creative efforts, to a general American "public discourse." The author's response to the temper of the sixties, therefore, was not a repudiation, but a *resituation,* of the self. Having always written from an autobiographical perspective, he suddenly discovered that his personal story was but part of a larger tale. The black writer's embattled struggle for fulfillment in America, he came to imply, was a recapitulation of the quest of all black Americans for expressive wholeness.

The novel *If Beale Street Could Talk* clarifies this interpretation of Baldwin's most recent stipulations in aesthetics.[26] Fonny, the protagonist, is a sculptor. He not only hews figures like the one of a black man in pain struggling to escape an entrapping block of wood, but also shares a tender love affair with Tish, the young black woman who serves as the novel's narrator. The result of Tish and Fonny's relationship is a baby conceived in the artist's studio. New life, new images originating (as do the lovers themselves) from the black American masses—this is what Baldwin portrays. And the resulting picture constitutes a radical revision of his earlier definitions of black art and the black artist. Baldwin, as a socially responsible black spokesman, goes home to Harlem with *Beale Street.* And words from *No Name in the Street* show the sharply altered perspective he had to adopt in order to blend his voice with those of other blacks calling for a new world during the sixties and early seventies: "For the necessity, now, which I think nearly all black people see in different ways, is the creation and protection of a nucleus which will bring into existence a new people" (*No Name,* p. 166). The novelist's adoption of the point of view of the black American masses is, to me, the most notable fact of *Beale Street*'s production. The history of the black artist (Fonny) also serves as a chronicle of a people seeking freedom through their unique creativity.

One other renowned black author who remained active during the sixties was Ralph Ellison. Though he was usually omitted from the hagiology of creative artists compiled by his younger black contemporaries, he produced essays during the decade that enriched the black American literary tradition. An exacting formalism was Ellison's response to the turbulent social climate of the sixties and seventies. Unlike Baldwin, he found artistic noninvolvement a rather attractive status. In his later essays, he merely elevated what was in his early expositions a mediating realm (art) to the status of a primary and absolute existence. In doing so, he constructed for himself a refuge from the demands of the black liberation struggle and a fortress against the assaults of white, liberal critics like Irving Howe, who insisted that all black writers had to model their work on the writings of Richard Wright.[27]

Ellison says an everlasting No to both camps in *Shadow and Act*. The tenor of his aesthetics is reflected by the following lines from "Hidden Name and Complex Fate":

> It is a matter of outrageous irony, perhaps, but in literature the great social clashes of history no less than the painful experience of the individual are secondary to the meaning which they take on through the skill, the talent, the imagination and personal vision of the writer who transforms them into art. Here they are reduced to more manageable proportions; here they are imbued with humane value; here, injustice and catastrophe become less important in themselves than what the writer makes of them. [*Shadow and Act*, pp. 148–49]

Ellison thus posits a dichotomy between literature and "the great social clashes of history." This means that critics who wish to assess a literary work must approach it from an evaluative stance in aesthetics and not from an ideological posture in social ethics. Art is not sociology and must not be treated as though it were. Ellison argues the point at great length in "The World and the Jug."His conclusions are intended not only for white critics who attempt to set boundaries on the field of black literature, but also for black activists: "no Negroes are beating down my door, putting pressure on me to join the Negro Freedom Movement, for the simple reason that they realize that I am enlisted for the duration . . . my Negro friends recognize a certain division of labor among the members of the tribe. Their demands, like that of many whites, are that I publish more novels—and here I am remiss and vulnerable perhaps" (*Shadow and Act*, p. 147). One has only the author's word that no blacks troubled his door. But it can be safely inferred that had any bothered to knock, calling him to a more overt form of social action, they would have been roundly denied.

A mass conversion of older black writers did not occur during the sixties and seventies. But most of those from earlier generations did respond to the new demands of the era. The black artist had allied himself with a black majority, and in some cases the artist assumed a leadership role. Baraka, for example, virtually organized the mayoral campaign of Richard Gibson in Newark, and countless others (like Sonia Sanchez, Askia Touré, and Haki Madhubuti) engaged in activities ranging from community-based creative writing workshops to the establishment of black studies programs at colleges and universities like San Francisco State. Major newspapers, including the *Washington Post* and the *New York Times*, carried long features on the Black Arts Movement. By the late sixties, the importance of the black artist—the writer in particular—had become an accepted fact for groups and individuals bent on a revolutionary change in American society. One result of this increased popularity was a heightened effort to make the works of black spokesmen available. New journals such as *Soul Book*, the *Journal of Black Poetry*, *Black Books Bulletin*, the *Black Scholar*, *Liberator* magazine, and scores of others were created in order to disseminate the word of those who were projecting a new world. Foremost here was *Negro Digest*, edited by Hoyt Fuller of Chicago. The name change which *Negro Digest* underwent during the sixties captured the spirit of the times: it was retitled *Black World*. Beyond periodicals dedicated to the work of artists and scholars, there were new black-owned-and-managed publishing companies that provided impetus for the movement. In the Midwest, Third-World Press, the Free Black Press, and Dudley Randall's incomparable Broadside Press were established. Broadside was the most singular venture in black publishing of the past two decades. Its initial support came from Randall's personal bank account. To date, the press (which has changed ownership) has published hundreds of black poets and critics. In the East, Drum and Spear Press of Washington, D.C., and Baraka's Jihad Productions came into existence.

By the early seventies, there was unprecedented demand

for black writing. And given one of the basic rules of American book publishing, i.e., commerce follows demand, it seems superfluous to point out that large white publishing firms were soon involved in the production and distribution of books by black authors. Booksellers who had scarcely given a thought to black works filled their shelves with the writings of Wright, Ellison, Baldwin, Baraka, and others. Not only were older titles reissued, some of which had lain dormant for years, but works by unknown black writers were solicited by major publishers.

The black writer, it seemed, had come of age, and editors like Hoyt Fuller proclaimed a "New Black Renaissance." The only precedent for contemporary creative impulses appeared to be that flurry of artistic activity among black Americans of the 1920s called the "Harlem Renaissance." A great deal has changed since such views were first postulated, and today most of those who spoke so confidently have found it imperative to reevaluate the artistic and critical acts of the sixties and seventies. Though many were aware, even before the mid-seventies, that the ebullience of black nationalist politics and art was premature, the actual effects of the recent florescence of black nationalism have yet to be analyzed. It is easy to isolate the deficiencies and excesses of the sixties and early seventies. It is more difficult, however, to render a precise view of the accomplishments of the era. One of its achievements stands out clearly: the redefinition of black writing and the role of the writer. The creative works of a generation often outlive the memory of even its most stirring sociopolitical acts. At this time, when the passionate proclamations of black national sovereignty have become whimpers, the works of contemporary black literature serve as agencies of renewal. They remain as a testimony to the difficult journey undertaken and the revised terms for order that have been its result.

Any assessment of the black nationalist impulse in recent years must begin by acknowledging that the accuracy of such a prospect has always been at issue. There has always been a retreat from the details of the journey when presented from such a standpoint. Normally, the writer is accused of intemperance, exaggeration, or falsification by rational men and women who have agreed out of fear to ignore the irrationalities of the social fabric encompassing them. Their reaction is also condoned by the infinitely human wish to correlate the world of dream with that of human actualities. For societies of men and women, as Baldwin notes, are held together by an uneasy, but firm, consensus that anything militating against the status quo should be eliminated. For the writer to face the full force and implications of chaos and disruption is thus to court criticism, contempt, and perhaps his own destruction. And yet it is only through such encounters that he comes to understand who and what he is.

In black America, the urge toward an uncritical acceptance of the larger society has always been counterpointed by energetic voices suggesting an alternative course. Fifteen years after Forten's letter, the following words came from a freeman of Charleston, South Carolina: "If you do go [to Liberia], and I hope in my heart all of us [black people] may speedily go—will we not go with our families and friends; cementing more strongly the bond of our connections, our customs, and our habits? Look for example to the Jews and other ancient people, scattered over the world; look at our situation, wherever we are placed: we see no innovation, nothing likely to break in and change the existing face of society."[28] Clearly, "home" for the writer of this passage was not the middle ground of America. His perspective on both the present and the future stands in marked contrast to Forten's. The key words are "no innovation, nothing likely to break in and change the existing face of society." But one might infer a qualification: society can be decisively altered by informed action on the part of black people themselves.

Trained to silence and subservience by the white world around them, blacks have sometimes left the specification of terms for order to others. There have always been those, however, like the writers treated up to now and the South Carolinian here in question, who have insisted on speech and action in their own behalf. The overriding assumption on the part of such spokesmen has been that African life, black American culture, and black men and women in society contain values that must be preserved, fostered, and communicated. The result of their labors has been the kind of resistance to white definitions discussed earlier and the retention and development of distinctive terms in a black encyclopedia of meanings. To bring all one knows to an understanding of the human condition is, for the black writer, to bring unique fields of meaning and value.

And within these distinctive areas there lies the virtual, or incipient, possibility that the fundamental opposition between black and white in America is an irreconcilable one. In the presence of conditions suggested by this possibility, black spokesmen have often cast aside such linguistic strategies as the restrained tone of discourse seen in Wheatley and Vassa, the proclamation of patriotism represented by Forten, and the tacit agreement between black and white ideals that one can infer from the autobiographical acts of Douglass and Washington. They have substituted for such strategies a direct, unmediated discourse addressed to a black audience and asserting ideals in harmony with what they claim as an accurate black historical perspective.

As early as 1773, four black men of Massachusetts made it clear that they did not expect any significant innovation in American life as they then knew it: "We are willing to submit to such regulations and laws as may be made relative to us, until we leave the province, which we determine to do as soon as we can from our joynt labours procure money to transport ourselves to some part of the coast of Africa, where we propose a settlement."[29] For both the freeman of Charleston and the black spokesmen from Massachusetts, Africa was more than a faraway green light. Rather than an idealized homeland in the distant past or in a dreamed afterlife, it was a physical territory, a place of the immediate future.

Given the black situation in America, these writers advocated repatriation to Africa as the one hope for black independence and full human rights. Martin Delany also had emigration in mind in 1852, when he wrote:

> What the unfortunate classes are in Europe, such are we in the United States, which is folly to deny, insanity not to understand, blindness not to see, and surely now full time that our eyes were opened to these startling truths, which for ages

> have stared us full in the face.... Have we not now sufficient intelligence among us to understand our true position, to realise our actual condition, and determine for ourselves what is best to be done? If we have not now, we never shall have, and should at once cease prating about our equality, capacity, and all that... our elevation must be the result of *self-efforts,* and work of our *own hands.* No other human power can accomplish it. If we but determine it shall be so, it will be so. Let each one make the case his own, and endeavor to rival his neighbor, in honorable competition.[30]

Delany did not single out Africa as the place of immigration, however. He believed South and Central America were more desirable since blacks had established their rights to the Western Hemisphere by dint of long service and heroic sacrifice. Like the freemen already mentioned, he had discovered the irreconcilability of black manhood and white American life. He too was anxious that a separation be immediately effected in order to allow the full worth and dignity of black life to flourish. And he did not hesitate to summon up realities that most in his society were content to ignore: "Our desire is, to arrest the attention of the American people in general, and the colored people in particular, to great truths as heretofore but little thought of" (*Condition,* p. 51).

The most salient truths, for Delany, were the superiority of Africans in the arts of civilization and the general inferiority and greed of Europeans (*Condition,* pp. 62–63). His first injunction, then, was for Africans in America to survey a historical background different from the one traditionally held out to view. Second, he urged blacks to withdraw from the American land of oppression. The Fugitive Slave Law of 1850, which made it illegal for any state in the country to harbor an escaped slave, offers the most striking evidence for Delany of the role that America ascribes to black people in general. The language of the law included the following: "In no trial or hearing under this act shall the testimony of such alleged fugitive [from service or labor] be admitted in evidence." At all costs, Delany felt, blacks had to flee from this position of mute servitude.

Prior to Delany's discourse, David Walker's *Appeal* of 1829 had sketched a solution nearer at hand. Like that group of slaves who, according to the historian Herbert Aptheker, revolted in 1526, all black men and women, according to Walker, should rise up and throw off the yoke of a specifically American oppression. To stand still while one was slowly murdered constituted, in Walker's view, the act of a heathenish infidel. God himself ordained that a true Christian should be free, even if it meant slitting the throat of his oppressors in order to be so.

The writings mentioned so far are unmediated; they are addressed directly "to the coloured people of the world, but in particular and very expressly to those of the United States of America." And in 1940, W. E. B. Du Bois had the same audience in mind when he wrote:

> With its eyes open to the necessity of agitation and to possible migration, this plan [for full Negro rights and Negro equality in America] would start with the racial grouping that today is inevitable and proceed to use it as a method of progress along which we have worked and are now working. Instead of letting this segregation remain largely a matter of chance and unplanned development, and allowing its objects and results to rest in the hands of the white majority or in the accidents of the situation, it would make the segregation a matter of careful thought and intelligent planning on the part of Negroes.[31]

What Du Bois champions is a strategy of economic communalism among black Americans. Such a plan is in harmony with what he sees as a drastically changing world economy resulting from the "collapse of capitalism" (*Dusk of Dawn*, p. 198). The prime agents for such a plan are his addressees—black people: "The cost of this program must fall first and primarily on us, ourselves. It is silly to expect any large number of whites to finance a program which the overwhelming majority of whites today fear and reject" (*Dusk of Dawn*, p. 197). And where did Du Bois find auguries for success?

> In the African communal group, ties of family and blood, of mother and child, of group relationship, made the group leadership strong, even if not always toward the highest cul-

> ture. In the case of the more artificial group among American Negroes, there are sources of strength in common memories of suffering in the past; in present threats of degradation and extinction; in common ambitions and ideals; in emulation and the determination to prove ability and desert. Here in subtle but real ways the communalism of the African clan can be transferred to the Negro American group, implemented by higher ideals of human accomplishment through the education and culture which have arisen and may further arise through contact of black folk with the modern world. [*Dusk of Dawn,* p. 219]

To revolt, to leave, to withdraw to a separate and autonomous existence are also part of the journey back. Recognizing clearly the "threats of degradation and extinction," the assumption that blacks "owed" service or labor to white America, and the improbability that anything would alter the "existing face of society," the black spokesman has often granted his allegiance to the idea of a sovereign black nation—a single, unified body which takes responsibility for its own destiny. Collective black action guided by an exact black historical perspective are norms here. And the spokesman calls attention not to his or his people's similarity to white Americans, or Englishmen, or men in general, but to the distinctive features of black life.

For black art this course of action entails a repudiation of the situation captured by Du Bois: "Most whites want Negroes to amuse them; they demand caricature; they demand jazz; and torn between these allegiances: between the extraordinary reward for entertainers of the white world and meager encouragement to honest self-expression, the artistic movement among American Negroes has accomplished something, but it has never flourished and never will until it is deliberately planned" (*Dusk of Dawn,* pp. 202–3). Under the black nationalist prospect, the black spokesman is articulate not in the service of white amusement, but on behalf of the "elevation, emigration, and destiny of the colored people of the United States," to borrow Delany's words. Frederick Douglass once quipped, "I thank God for making me a man simply, but Delany always thanks Him for making him a black man." Abolitionist sentiments, promises of equality, and omnipresent assurances from the white world acted as stays for Douglass, but there have always been the assumptions of white supremacy and the threats of extinction to motivate Delany and others. What the black nationalist text offers is discourse that delineates these counterforces and suggests—directly to black people—an appropriate response. The contours of the journey are simply incomplete without the details supplied by such a text. Bishop Henry M. Turner, Marcus Garvey, and Malcolm X all knew this and joined the chorus of black nationalists who profoundly troubled their masters' quiet.

Baraka and other writers of the sixties and seventies, therefore, did not create ab nihilo. Neither the black nationalist prospect nor the type of text it inspires was indigenous to the past two decades. What was original and awesome in the florescence of nationalism of the past several years was the extent to which such a prospect and its text became norms among a vast segment of the black population. Du Bois lamented that whites were too often the intended audience for black art in the forties. And almost a hundred years earlier, Delany had complained about the reaction his own work was likely to receive from blacks:

> In presenting this work, we have but a single object in view, and this is, to inform the minds of the colored people at large, upon many things pertaining to their elevation, that but few among us are acquainted with. Unfortunately for us, as a body, we have been taught to believe, that we must have some person to think for us, instead of thinking for ourselves. So accustomed are we to submission and this kind of training, that it is with difficulty, even among the most intelligent of the colored people, an audience may be elicited for any purpose whatever, if the expounder is to be a colored person; and the introduction of any subject is treated with indifference, if not contempt, when the originator is a colored person. [*Condition*, p. 190]

During recent years, by contrast, there was little chance that the black masses would listen to a spokesman other than a black person. The increased literacy of the masses, combined with the black writer's conscious decision to create works that had mass appeal, was instrumental in a new unity that was inconceivable to Delany, and but a distant goal in the eyes of Du Bois. Some of the factors that account for this solidarity have been detailed above. The most important, it seems to me, was the ascendancy of the Third World. After Bandung, the informed writer of color anywhere in the world could no longer afford to ignore his peculiar situation in his own land. In black America, this meant a realization on the part of black spokesmen that they too were colonial subjects held in bondage by the force of world capitalism. Like the newly emergent nations of Asia, Africa, and the Caribbean, the black American nation had to seek ways within a unique set of meanings and values to become independent. In part, this required a return to the texts of black nationalist writers of the past. On a broader plane, it demanded a bold and far-reaching choice between alternatives. Could black spokesmen destroy altogether that urge to join the larger society that had always prevailed among black Americans? The assumption was that they could, and writers like Baraka set out to try.

The drama of the blacks' attempted self-liberation comprises another dimension of the total acculturation process. In the sixties and seventies, black spokesmen concluded that the competition between sets of meanings could be judged only if one fully understood what had kept white definitions in ascendance. Given the struggle to become articulate and to maintain distinctive semantic fields that has been discussed up to now, it is no surprise that contemporary spokesmen had access to a rather full arsenal of facts. There was a vigorous tradition which required contemplation. Some, like Baraka, simply assumed that the entire past of black writing had to be jettisoned ("The Myth of a Negro Literature"). Others, of less nihilistic bent, decided that the essential meanings of black culture were not to be found in literary works of art. The folk productions of black America—tales, songs, blues, jazz, oratory, and sermons—were considered the true repositories of value.

Larry Neal was working under this premise when he wrote:

> We can learn more about what poetry is by listening to the cadences in Malcolm's speeches, than from most of Western poetics. Listen to James Brown scream. Ask yourself, then: Have you ever heard a Negro poet sing like that? Of course not, because we have been tied to the texts, like most white poets. The text could be destroyed and no one would be hurt in the least by it. The key is in the music. Our music has always been far ahead of our literature. Actually, until recently, it was our only literature, except for, perhaps, the folktale.[32]

Neal thus moves to reinstate a concept from folkloristics—performance. He insists that the black spokesman must "take his work where his people are: Harlem, Watts, Philadelphia, Chicago and the rural South. He must learn to embellish the context in which the work is executed; and where possible, link the work to all usable aspects of the music. For the context of the work is as important as the work itself. Poets must learn to sing, dance and chant their works, tearing into the substance of their individual and collective experiences."[33]

The text, transmitted as performance, is a public occasion (like that seen in Brooks's "The Wall"), rather than a private act of literacy. It is a ritual statement of the solidarity and continuity of a culture; it takes its place among other transmissions and elaborations of culture such as weddings, festivals, funerals, and so on. As such, it has a register[34] different from the ones traditionally specified for literary texts. The field of the black cultural performance is public interaction, and its mode is song or chant. The tenor is communal—a voice addressing an entire group in ceremonial ways. The writer thus becomes an active tradition bearer,[35] rather than a passive craftsman pursuing meaning alone in his workshop.

Another way of characterizing this is to say that in recent years black spokesmen became popular entertainers directing their performances to a black audience. The success of the enterprise was demonstrated by the hundreds of thousands of copies of his books that a poet like Haki Madhubuti was able to sell to black people. Further evidence was offered by the mass black audiences that turned out for readings by black authors in Harlem, Philadelphia, Washington, D.C, and elsewhere. And the most convincing evidence of all was provided by the kinds of literary works that black people from all walks of life began to demand from publishers, newsstands, and college professors. It did indeed seem as though black literature had found its communal voice and that its writers had contributed to a radical modification of the acculturative process—a modification that allowed black meanings to move into the foreground.

But slightly more than a decade later, one discovers an eerie silence from the black nationalist camp, or at best a low, perplexed voice wondering what has gone wrong. The familiar process of black victims blaming themselves for their victimization is well underway in 1979. If the black nationalist prospect and the texts it entails have been forced into the background, however, it is possible that the Law Enforcement Assistance Administration, which grew out of the Omnibus Crime Control and Safe Streets Act of 1968, was enormously influential in the process.[36] The agency's budget, which was designed for distribution to state and local police, increased from $63 million in 1968 to $1.73 billion in 1973.[37] Most of this money was spent for the type of upgrading mentioned earlier: police forces became internal, paramilitary regiments.

There was also the Federal Bureau of Investigation's order set down by J. Edgar Hoover in 1971. Titled "Counterintelligence Program, Internal Security, Disruption of the New Left," the communication said: "We must frustrate every effort of these groups and individuals [the New Left, particularly 'black extremists'] to consolidate their forces or to recruit new and faithful adherents."[38] A wave of repression swept over America, resulting in strategic arrests of some black spokesmen and the wanton murder of others. The campaign was sanctioned by the highest governmental offices in America and was aided by "faithful adherents" in the Central Intelligence Agency. It was a given among most white Americans that blacks were not to be allowed to speak and act in their own behalf. White publishers, following the instinct of the no-longer-demanding herd, declared that the "black market" was closed.

If silence obtains, therefore, there are reasons beyond the failings of black spokesmen that help to account for it. One causal factor that remains unexplored, for example, is the recruitment and training, in colleges and universities, of a black neocolonial élite. In 1965, there were 210,000 blacks between the ages of eighteen and twenty-four enrolled in the academy; by 1970, there 416,000. For a brief period, young black men and women were troubling voices in higher education, but as the current generation of black students pursues its studies, the general American situation and the state of academe seem in harmony. An enforced passivity and fear in American society in general are matched by black uncertainty and quiescence within the academy. Articulate young blacks who might have played significant roles in the black community have been effectively removed. Their training in the academy makes it unlikely that they will ever return home. Of course, this is not the same as insisting that the "young warriors" have been coopted from the black community. It is (to return to Wright's statements discussed earlier) simply an ironical realization that the ways of colonialism are subtle indeed. To draw off the young, to place them in institutions that alienate them from their culture, has a devastating impact on the growth of any nation. And the type of literacy guaranteed by the academy today is still not calculated to provide anything approaching an adequate definition of black life in America. Instead, the university remains a bastion of racism, complacency, and incompetence, striving desperately to maintain the status quo. It is no surprise, therefore, that the majority of black students in such institutions seldom find their way to courses devoted to rigorous analysis of their own culture, or come, in those crucial years of preadulthood, to any sense of themselves as representatives of a unique culture. White America has spent billions of dollars and a great amount of repressive energy to ensure the dominance of white meanings.

It is impossible to situate the efforts of recent black writers outside this context and to assume the black nationalist prospect fell away exclusively as a result of its own shortcomings. On the contrary, at no time in the history of black America have so many spokesmen dedicated themselves, in serious and informed ways, to a particular set of meanings and values. These men and women altered the existing face of society in a way that makes it impossible to begin the journey back as though blacks have always rushed eagerly into the harbors of the white world. The texts of the sixties and seventies constitute a level of discourse where functional oppositions are readily observable. Upon their performance, *by the reader,* they signal the unique values of a sui generis tradition, and an understanding of Baraka's contemporaneity, for example, leads to an apprehension of the black past as a whole:

> Calling black people
> Calling all black people, man woman child
> Wherever you are, calling you, urgent, come in
> Black People, come in, wherever you are, urgent, calling
> you, calling all black people
> calling all black people, come in, black people, come
> on in.
>
> [*Black Magic,* p. 115]

5 The Black Spokesman as Critic: Reflections on the Black Aesthetic

During the sixties and seventies, the black spokesman's mass constituency issued its own call; it demanded loud, insistent, and comprehensible voices. The eminence of black writers and critics during the era was a result of their willingness to provide such voices. An entire culture seemed on the move toward a resplendent future. To speed the day, black spokesmen addressed themselves—in the strident, generalized tones that became de rigueur—to almost every conceivable issue. Seeking a form of discourse that had mass appeal, they arrived at the kind of verbal structures specified by Larry Neal and discussed in the preceding chapter. Attempting to eradicate what they considered the lies of history, they made forays into all areas of social, political, and artistic life.

The margins for confusion under these conditions were, obviously, quite wide. Not only were there powerful and contradictory pressures from white America at work—with its promises of equality on the one hand and its threats of extinction on the other—but there were also urgent demands from black Americans for forceful truths that would lead to a new world. These were difficult straits to negotiate, and there was little time for the kind of reflection that ensures a flawless passage. The necessity was to continue speaking in a manner that both counteracted the repressions of the white world and clarified the black situation for those who shared it.

The complexity of such a stance is emblematic of black American intellectual history. For to act "appropriately" may well be to storm the barricades of the white world with the intention of destroying a long-standing enemy. But black spokesmen have always been aware of the immense and subtle power wielded by those on the other side of the barricades. How, then, could they assume that what Amiri Baraka has called "instructions for black people" were easy to construct or articulate?

The answer is that this assumption has seemed operative only during periods of extreme social agitation like the past decades. It was not a lack of analytical ability or a naive faith in the imminence of change that prompted both the form and the content of the black spokesman's utterances during recent years, but rather a self-conscious desire to both shape and satisfy the requirements of an epoch. If we now find fault with many of the black American utterances of our recent past and explain the decline of contemporary black nationalist efforts as the result of indigenous failings, it is only because we possess the assured wisdom of hindsight. There were, to be sure, shortcomings among black spokesmen, but it is a mistake to ascribe them to either a lack of intelligence or a paucity of imagination. One does not heed trivial missteps of the past; they are quickly forgotten. Our attention is continually arrested, however, by historical objects and events that seem to augur a new order of society. The "Black Aesthetic" represented this kind of cultural manifestation. In the realm of literary criticism, it represented one of the most striking instances of the construction of a prospect for the times by black spokesmen.[1]

And the times were idealistic. There was thus a propensity on the part of the spokesmen for the Black Aesthetic to employ a form of utterance that occurs time and again in the fictive discourse of Booker T. Washington. Just as Washington attempted to bring a utopian world into existence by verbal fiat, so have many recent black critics attempt *to will* into being a new art and criticism. The mode adopted by these critics might therefore be called *conative,* and their speech acts might be called *conative utterances.*[2] Several examples drawn from contemporary criticism will help to clarify my claims.

I use the concept of the "afterimage" (visual images that remain after a stimulus has passed) to situate the following illustrations in the domain of perception. The first instance is drawn from *Black Fire, An Anthology of Afro-American Writing,* edited by Baraka and Neal and published in 1968. The volume's foreword, written by Baraka, begins: "These [writers whose work appears in the collection] are the founding Fathers and Mothers, of our nation. We rise, as we rise again. By the power of our beliefs, by the purity and strength of our actions." And it closes: "The black artist. The black man. The holy holy black man. The man you seek. The climber the striver. The maker of peace. The lover. The warrior . . . . We are presenting, from God, a tone, your own. Go on. Now."[3] I interpret these statements as conative utterances. The goal they propose is rebirth. But the rebirth represented is an exclusively lexical one: the words strive to recreate a primordial black logos, or word, through sheer lyricism and assertiveness. God, the artist, and the "holy holy black man" are possible agents of a new creation, but underlying their mention is the tacit premise that words are primary realities. The reborn "nation," it would appear, is a function of words conceived as substance or essence. Baraka's utterances stand alone as the significant actors. The key terms of his discourse are "actions," "seek," "presenting," "rise," "founding." The title *Black Fire* and the iconic sign constituted by the anthology's dust jacket provide some idea of the stimulus that motivated the foreword. The jacket hurls bold, flaming, black capitals at the reader like Molotov cocktails. The conflagration and disorder of Harlem, Watts, Newark, and other black urban centers were, in fact, primary experiences. *Black Fire* and its packaging are governed by afterimages. The implications of this heuristic assertion become clearer in the light of two additional examples.

In the year that *Black Fire* appeared, Larry Neal issued his frequently reprinted manifesto, "The Black Arts Movement." The essay begins:

> The Black Arts Movement is radically opposed to any concept of the artist that alienates him from his community. Black Art is the aesthetic and spiritual sister of the Black Power concept. As such, it envisions an art that speaks directly to the needs and aspirations of Black America. In order to perform this task, The Black Arts Movement proposes a radical reordering of the Western cultural aesthetic. It proposes a separate symbolism, mythology, critique, and iconology. The Black Arts and the Black Power concept both relate broadly to the Afro-American's desire for self-determination and nationhood. Both concepts are nationalistic. One is concerned with the relationship between art and politics; the other with the art of politics.[4]

"Desire," "proposes," "perform," "radical reordering" are terms that mark what I call the conative mode. They communicate Neal's desire to alter existing structures to accord with the wishes of black America. Like Baraka's, Neal's statements are characterized by the absence of words that point to specific agents, events, or strategies. The phrase, "Black Arts Movement," occupies the stage alone—proposing, performing, speaking, and so on. Its words do not point to any tangible referent, and this is a direct result of the statement's being grounded in afterimages.

A specific set of social events comprised the original stimulus. On a sweltering southern night, a rapt black audience was moved to a call-and-response chant in which the appropriate response was "Black Power." There followed a storm of political fury and debate that remains to be analyzed. Neal's text fails even to hint at the complexity one might infer from the ongoing intellectual history of the sixties and early seventies. His utterances simply establish, by will and assertion, a family resemblance ("aesthetic and spiritual sister") between two phrases ("Black Art" and "Black Power"), both of which remain vague. The value of the critic's discourse is commensurate with the specificity of its governing percepts. And afterimages are notoriously lacking in precision and detail.

Three years after Neal's pronouncement, Addison Gayle published an anthology of critical essays called *The Black Aesthetic*. Gayle's definition of the Black Aesthetic furnishes a third example:

> The question for the black critic today is not how beautiful is a melody, a play, a poem, or a novel, but how much more beautiful has the poem, melody, play, or novel made the life of a single black man? The Black Aesthetic, then, as conceived by this writer, is a corrective—a means of helping black people out of the polluted mainstream of Americanism, and offering logical, reasoned, arguments as to why he [*sic*] should not desire to join the ranks of a Norman Mailer or a William Styron.[5]

Here the afterimages were cued by glossy posters and lapel buttons of the sixties and seventies that portrayed idealized African and black American figures. Their captions were always the same: Black is Beautiful. The key word in Gayle's passage is "beautiful." An act of synonymy provides the more abstract "aesthetic" and projects the passage into the literary critical domain. The mode is still actional. The Black Aesthetic helps, corrects, offers, and transforms. But like Baraka's reborn "nation," and Neal's Black Arts Movement, Gayle's Black Aesthetic resides in an isolated context constituted by desire alone. No realistic plan of action or analysis emerges. For the logical import of their motivating afterimages places Gayle's remarks beyond the realm of tangible actions and events.

Obviously, these examples were not chosen at random. They were selected from the work of three of the more eminent spokesmen in contemporary black American literary criticism. Taken as representative discourse, they illustrate the distressingly limited amount of information conveyed by conative utterances. Such speech acts fail as analytical statements because their speakers substitute will for reason, volition for analysis, and desire for systematic observation. These transpositions stand Freud on his head, suggesting that where ego was, id should be. As a verbal act governed by willful inversion, conative discourse is a world that includes Blake's "The Marriage of Heaven and Hell," Nietzsche's *Thus Spake Zarathustra,* Kant's critiques, and the orations of Milton's Satan. The black American examples cited in this discussion all share with such classics of Western thought the tacit assumption that the human mind is its own place and can of itself make a hell out of heaven, a heaven out of hell. While this may be indisputable, it certainly raises awesome problems in the realm of the psychology of perception. Perception that moves in a purely volitional manner is scarcely perception at all. It is, instead, a mental operation that unceasingly confirms the superior status of desire. It is continually behind, beyond, or outside the facts of primary human experience. Preferring residual effects, it strives to restructure the world on the basis of volition alone.

To a greater extent than most will acknowledge, the history of black American literary criticism is rooted in the conative mode. The critical canon is filled with statements by men and women whose conceptions of black literature have been guided by idealism and desire rather than by general analytic notions that can be fruitfully applied to the study of literature. The black literary text, that is to say, has been continually evaluated in ways that have forced it into harmony with various idealizations of the world. One has only to turn to the writings of, say, Benjamin Brawley, Alain Locke, Richard Wright, Ralph Ellison, or Margaret Just Butcher to see this procrustean endeavor at first hand.[6] The formulations of these authors reveal ofttimes anguished efforts to structure reality to fit the bedrock of a splendid idealism. Brawley, for example, used genteel, Victorian criteria in discussing black literature during a time when black Americans were constantly subjected to violence and terror. And while the masses of black America were suffering the oppression of lynchings and economic deprivation during the 1920s, Locke exuberantly proclaimed the birth of a "New Negro." Civil rights workers were being arrested, beaten, and murdered when Wright predicted a harmonious American society in which black life and literature would flow peacefully into the white mainstream. Finally, Butcher and Ellison could have been prompted only by idealism when they thought of black American literature under the conditions of a *genuinely* pluralistic American society.

Idealism, conation alone, it seems to me, has been a compelling force in the work of the black American literary critic. It has led him to assign such arbitrary classifications to black literary texts as political index, certificate of cultivation, personal chronicle, philosophical treatise, propaganda, and so on. Terms like slave narrative, novel, and autobiography, have been employed, on occasion, simply as higher-order substitutes. A case can be made for any one of these names. But the appropriate response, at this instant in the history of black literary criticism, is not to name (or to rename) black literary texts on the basis of some idealistic, sociopolitical vision of the world. The job before the present-day analyst is to study the expressive manifestations of black American culture in ways that allow one to interpret such works as structured creativity that derives its meanings from a rich cultural context.

There are reasons for calling attention to the present moment in black literary criticism. The statements of Baraka, Neal, and Gayle, while they are characteristic of utterances from the general domain of black literary criticism, must be distinguished from works of earlier black American critics. This distinction can be made on the basis of audience considerations alone, since the statements of recent spokesmen for the Black Aesthetic have been received by a sizable black audience. The emergence of such an audience was but a fond hope of black America less than three decades ago. Access to an education approximating that available to whites became de jure for blacks only in 1954. Behind this year lies what W. E. B. Du Bois describes as the steep mountain path to Canaan—the agonizing and legally impassable road to black literacy. During the years since 1954, as I suggested in the preceding chapter, the increasing literacy of black America has forced artists and critics to consider the possible effects of their utterances under conditions dictated by a black response.

The effective use of a term like Black Aesthetic presupposes a black population that can give rise to two interpretants of the term *literate*—i.e., "literary" and "familiar with literature." To spur black Americans to action by means of the written, conative utterance, that is to say, presupposes a literate black population. And the goal of modifying this group's sense of literary works of art presupposes its familiarity with literature. When these presuppositions were realized during the last two decades, they created a context for the black spokesman's use of the Black Aesthetic as a poetic construct. This phrase and others like it were suddenly capable of carrying an emotive force not unlike that of poetry. They called attention to themselves, producing an interest on the part of black readers that motivated a search for analytical means of describing, disproving, or validating what the utterances only willed or asserted.

In their positive manifestations, then, conative utterances such as *Black Aesthetic* and *Black Arts Movement* are products of the black critic as artist. During their utterance, the spokesman is a figure equivalent to James Weldon Johnson's creator. Stepping out on space, he says: "I'll make me a world." This simple volitional statement does not analyze the creative process, nor does it describe the salient features of the world proposed. It does, however, signal the fact that a sui generis world is, at least, imaginable. Since so many advocates for the Black Aesthetic have been creative writers and artists, they have often proposed a world of independent black creativity and criticism. Their proposed world is usually represented as a place of dedicated black artists and an engaged black audience capable of conscious response to striking works of black art.

And when a number of contemporary spokesmen agreed that black artists required men and women in their own image to authenticate their efforts, the Black Aesthetic also became a critical slogan. Sloganizing is a familiar practice in literary criticism, and it is normally an ex post facto process. Wordsworth, for example, described the function of "lyrical ballads" after his and Coleridge's poems were ready for publication. And T. S. Eliot proclaimed a "dissociated sensibility" and an "objective correlative" after he had discovered certain tendencies at work in the canons of British literature. Similarly, black spokesmen announced the Black Aesthetic after the artistic awareness and the audience developments just discussed manifested themselves as new orders of phenomena in black America. The Black Aesthetic, then, was at a very fundamental level an articulation of a point of view in aesthetics.

Artists (regardless of race, creed, color, or place of national origin) are compelled at the beginning of their work to pose the question, Is there anybody there? This is what Delany and Du Bois had in mind when they speculated on the function of black art and the composition of its ideal audience. There is more involved here, however, than a question of the rigidly specified group to which an artist appeals. As soon as audience considerations are introduced, one is confronted with a fascinating array of issues. What, for example, compels a writer to render his personal, private, instinctual experiences in a form accessible to others? Any theory of aesthetics must treat this question as fundamental. It is, finally, an inquiry into the mode of existence—the ontology—of the work of art itself. Among black American writers, questions of the ontology of the work of art have always been integrally bound to queries about the ontology of black Americans. The black writer, as the foregoing discussions of language and acculturation imply, has occupied a complex situation. According to Christopher Caudwell, and Ezekiel Mphahlele who follows Caudwell's lead in *Voices in the Whirlwind,* it is a cultural collectivity that validates, or confirms, the existence of both the writer and his works of art.[7]

The status of black America as a collectivity, however, has always been correlated with harsh codes designed by white America to ensure its power over black Americans. As a consequence of this state of affairs, there was, for all too long, no tangible, literate, accessible black collectivity to answer the black writer's query, Is there anybody there? There were only whites intent on cultural hegemony. There was only what has come to be called the white literary critical establishment engaged in a discourse built on the prevailing, publicly articulated, white notions of black America. Questions of artistic form, judgment, and effect all seemed to have been answered by a white "other" when Wheatley compiled her *Poems on Various Subjects, Religious and Moral,* and perhaps too when Ellison wrote the enigmatic concluding sentence for *Invisible Man:* "Who knows but that, on the lower frequencies, I speak for you?" The urge toward the larger society (so strong in black America) has continually worked against the black spokesman's attempt to produce works that analyze or appeal to a black cultural collectivity. Addison Gayle expresses this as follows:

> The black artist of the past worked with the white public in mind. The guidelines by which he measured his production was its acceptance or rejection by white people. To be damned by a white critic and disavowed by a white public was reason enough to damn the artist in the eyes of his own people. The invisible censor, white power, hovered over him in the sanctuary of his private room—whether at the piano or the typewriter—and, like his black brothers, he debated about what he could say to the world without bringing censure upon himself.[8]

There was, however, always someone present in addition to whites, someone very dark of hue and experience. There was a resonant black culture, with its own music and poetry, its own sacred texts and sculpted images. This collectivity could not respond to the black writer's question because the forms in which it was placed were not accessible. Until the writer's forms were designed to fit the collectivity's needs, or until the nature of the collectivity was altered forever by formal education, or until black artists awakened to a sense of a nearly irretrievable loss of contact with their culture and its primary artistic forms, the audience determining black creativity was destined to be conceived of by the black artist as a bland generality known as white America. Formal education has come; traditional forms (such as the folk products mentioned by Neal) have been scrutinized for their adaptability, and contemporary black American artists have undertaken the journey back. The process of determining the exact nature of the artist's "private" (i.e., authentic) experiences and how they can be most effectively communicated to a black audience, in other words, has gained tremendous impetus in recent years.

James Emanuel writes: "The black aesthetic, having at least a name, consequently has a past."[9] Like Ralph Ellison, Emanuel believes it is through our names that we place ourselves in the world. But the Black Aesthetic is not bound by a name. More than a simple, rhetorical strategy motivated by idealism, the phrase has served as a poetic construct, and as an artistic slogan raising substantive issues in aesthetics. An utterance of the phrase signals the black artist's awareness of a new role—a new mode of being for himself and his works of art. Implicit in its statement is a revised assessment of the function of black art. Literary theoreticians and critics have usually regarded the question of artistic function as one occasioning an analysis of the context in which works of art exist. This logical inference has led them to considerations of the purposes and effects of works of art in human societies—in relationship, that is to say, to the lives of various cultures. The Black Aesthetic, in its various usages and effects, has given to a newly realized black collectivity and its artists a sense of holism, a sense of an essential reciprocity between black art and black culture. In recent years, there has been not only a black audience awaiting the works of black artists, but also an energetic group of scholars whose works in black aesthetics have assured that the black spokesmen need never again suffer the isolation of the past. Black aesthetics—analytical inquiries into the nature, mode of existence, and evaluation of black art—is a reality, as even a cursory glance at such works as Stephen Henderson's *Understanding the New Black Poetry*, Addison Gayle's *The Way of the New World*, George Kent's *Blackness and the Adventure of Western Culture*, Shirley Ann Williams's *Give Birth to Brightness*, Arnold Rampersad's *The Art and Imagination of W. E. B. Du Bois*, and Dexter Fisher and Robert Stepto's *Afro-American Literature: The Reconstruction of Instruction* will show. And the entire complex of issues in aesthetics brought to public view by the conative utterance *Black Aesthetic* provided the constitutive conditions for such works and signaled (without equivocation) the context that gives them force.

6 *Black Creativity and American Attitudes*

There is consensus among scholars of black aesthetics that one goal of their analyses should be the isolation and clarification of relationships between white American attitudes and white American evaluations of black creativity. The writings of Vernon Parrington, D. H. Lawrence, Van Wyck Brooks and others have long since demolished an image of the rough-clad American innocent turning out doggerel stanzas and political tracts for the time. The observations of these scholars offer sufficient evidence to demonstrate the complexity of American intellectual history as manifested in literature and art. From more recent efforts like the writings of Alfred Kazin, Tony Tanner, Harry Levin, Leslie Fiedler, David Levin, Richard Chase, and Sacvan Bercovitch, one receives an even clearer sense of a serious, brooding intellect as the generative source of American literature. Few scholars, however, have analyzed the discrete statements of various white spokesmen that reflect American views of black creativity. C. Vann Woodward, Winthrop Jordan, George Fredrickson, and John Hope Franklin offer singular examples of historians who have insightfully explicated such statements. But in the domain of literary criticism, the task of clarifying the connection between such utterances and general American views of black artistry has become a broad analytical goal only in recent years, and most decisively, it seems to me, among black American scholars. In view of the complexity of American intellectual history, it would be senseless to attempt in this chapter an exhaustive classification of American attitudes. A consideration of three broad categories of critical judgments, however, will suggest some of the conceptual structures that have governed past evaluations of black art and culture in America.

It seems fitting that a view of these categories begin with Jefferson, to whom I promised to return earlier in my first chapter. Jefferson was not only influential among early American statesmen, but also representative. Both his biographers and a recent literary critic, Jean Fagin Yellin, have pointed to the seminal role his ideas played in colonial America. Professor Yellin, for example, has persuasively argued that Jefferson's view of the black American in *Notes on the State of Virginia* acted as a paradigm for later writers such as John Pendleton Kennedy, William Gilmore Simms, and Herman Melville.[1] It is, however, the critical component of Jefferson's *Notes* that is of interest in the present discussion.

After lauding native Americans (Indians) for their simple art work, Jefferson says: "But never yet could I find that a black had uttered a thought above the level of plain narration; never see even an elementary trait of painting or sculpture."[2] A brief nod to black music is followed by the author's well-known remarks on Phillis Wheatley: "Religion indeed has produced a Phyllis Whately [*sic*]; but it could not produce a poet. The compositions published under her name are below the dignity of criticism. The heroes of the *Dunciad* are to her, as Hercules to the author of that poem." Jefferson continues with his less-quoted (but more interesting) tirade against the African writer Ignatius Sancho, whose letters were published in England in 1782: "his imagination is wild and extravagant, escapes incessantly from every restraint of reason and taste, and, in the course of its vagaries, leaves a tract of thought as incoherent and eccentric, as is the course of a meteor through the sky. His subjects should have led him to a process of sober reasoning: yet we find him always substituting sentiment for demonstration." While Jefferson admits Sancho "to the first place among those of his own colour who have presented themselves to the public judgment," he sets him at the bottom of the column when compared with white epistlers.

One can partially explain Jefferson's evaluations by noting that they are in accord with a Humean consensus. David Hume, and other thinkers in Britain and America during the eighteenth century, felt that the taste of an intelligent man was a sufficient critical guide to literary works of art. The light of a common reason, they insisted, would lead the person of wit and propriety to art that gracefully clothed nature and, as Pope has it, felicitously expressed what was oft thought. Given this prospect, it is not surprising that Jefferson was unable to appreciate the arts of black America. They certainly did not satisfy Pope's ideal. One can also understand the white statesman's conception of black artists as creatures of mere passion. First, he was anxious to prove to the French naturalists like Buffon that white Americans were equivalent to inhabitants of more "civilized" nations. The process of "negative identification," in which whites projected their "savage" and "barbaric" impulses onto blacks or Indians, was in motion.[3] We are civilized, Jefferson seems to say, because *they* are so savage. Second, if black slaves were indeed human creatures infused with the light of common reason, how could Jefferson justify his own own role as a slaveholder? How could he sanction those clauses in the Constitution that he helped to formulate that guaranteed a place for slavery in America? Wheatley's verse, the product of a remarkable slave, had to be ranked far below the works satirized in the *Dunciad* if the center of Jefferson's universe was to hold.

Sancho's letters, however, occasioned more difficulty. They are the creations of a man who, as a child, entered the household of the Duke of Montagu. A fortunate and refined product of a slave system, he was tutored by royalty, a friend of Garrick, and a subject for Gainsborough. If any man deserved a place in the consensus, it was surely Sancho. Jefferson, therefore, damns the black epistler's work with faint praise: he is the first of his race but last in the general lists. He goes on to cast suspicion on the originality of the black writer's letters, saying it would be difficult to prove "they have received amendment from no other hand." The coup de grace in the evaluation, however, is Jefferson's argument from blood: "The improvement of the blacks in body and mind, in the first instance of their mixture with the whites, has been observed by every one, and proves that their inferiority is not the effect merely of their condition of life." Sancho's "condition of life," according to a Humean prospect, was certainly conducive to a tasteful creativity. But without Anglo-Saxon blood in his veins, Jefferson implies, Sancho scarcely stands a chance. The case is finally proved "upon the pulses."

Hedged round by scientific, religious, and political theories that placed the Anglo-Saxon (particularly the European Anglo-Saxon) on the highest rung of the human ladder, Jefferson could articulate only the harshest judgment on creative works by blacks. As an empirical observer who believed human talent would show through regardless of "condition of life," he found the evidence of the black man's humanity lacking. When Benjamin Banneker—the black mathematician, surveyor, and compiler of almanacs—sent him examples of his work, Jefferson responded with the hope that more evidence of a similar kind would be forthcoming. The irony, of course, is that Banneker felt compelled to try to persuade a man whose responses were so deeply rooted in the public discourse of his age. The basic proposition of the colonial period's pattern of judgment might be stated, Blacks are not as "human" as whites, hence one should not expect from them worthy expressions of the human order, e.g., accomplished works of art. To move from the colonial to the middle period of American history brings a shift from this proposition to another which is less global in its exclusions.

The abolitionists and proslavery advocates of the nineteenth century represent a revised white American estimate of blacks. Both groups, either tacitly or explicitly, supported the notion that black Americans were human beings at a lower developmental stage (either moral or intellectual) than white adults. William Lloyd Garrison speaks as follows about Frederick Douglass's *Narrative:* "Mr. Douglass has very properly chosen to write his own narrative, in his own style, and according to the best of his ability, rather than to employ someone else . . . I am confident that it is essentially true in all its statements; that nothing has been set down in malice, nothing exaggerated, nothing drawn from the imagination" (*Narrative,* pp. ix–x). These words from the preface serve as an affidavit to the *Narrative*'s authenticity, and the act of prefacing an unknown author's work is common practice even today. But one can infer from Garrison's statement a tone of dominance, an attitude of superiority. Since Douglass had indeed written the *Narrative* himself and had assured Garrison long since of his integrity and imagination, why did the white abolitionist find it necessary to assume the mood of a stern father confessor? Perhaps he was motivated by the same impulses that forced him to try to keep Douglass from founding the *North Star* as an independent abolitionist newspaper. The white freedom fighter finally gave indisputable proof of his paternalism in 1851, when he cried out against Douglass's new, anti-Garrisonian stance: "There is roguery somewhere!"[4] As long as the fugitive slave was willing to draw his inspiration and even certain features of his own self-representation from the man who would not "retreat a single inch," all was well. But when Douglass showed that his ship was, indeed, compassed by reason, the white man's wrath was unequivocal.

Garrison left firmly in place the question mark behind the utterance, Am I not a man and your brother? He was capable of conceding brotherhood, granting to blacks the role of young, inexperienced siblings. The abolitionist viewpoint did, however, allow for blacks as full-fledged human beings capable of adult development. During the years of fervent abolitionism and Civil War, all evidence of black creative ability was welcomed and advertised by antislavery advocates in their public arguments for black liberation. Black American songs, verses, letters, and narratives were all considered effective proofs that Caliban should, after a reasonable apprenticeship, be granted the rights and privileges enjoyed by white adults.

The foregoing account simply specifies the form American racial theorizing took during a particular era and in relationship to a select domain of the black experience—i.e., black creativity. Slave narratives sold by the thousands; black spirituals and work songs were suddenly of great interest to whites. The pattern of judgment surrounding these manifestations of black genius, however, was normally the one represented by Garrison's response to Douglass. Considered unusual products of a developing race, some of the most accomplished nineteenth-century black writings (the *Narrative of the Life of Frederick Douglass,* for example) were allowed to go out of print soon after the Civil War. (Another example, this, of the laws of commerce and demand in American publishing.) The reason it is absurd to condemn the mild racialism of the abolitionists, however, is not far to seek. If the effects of their outlook were not always profitable for black creativity, they were certainly immensely beneficial for the black American's body and soul. The abolitionist framework, while it stressed a conditional black puerility, also called for an end to American slavery.

America's proslavery advocates, by contrast, argued a sometimes vitriolic case for an eternal black childhood and enslavement. According to this faction, blacks were an intermediate species between men and brutes; they could move in one direction only—toward the bestial. As arrested beings trapped at an infantile stage of development, blacks would always (according to slavery's defenders) require the protection of kind and long-suffering white masters. The countless aspersions cast on slave narratives and other forms of black art by these spokesmen indicate their reaction to the notion of black creativity. The point of view they expressed carried the day in American letters during the postbellum period. The following statement written by William Owens in 1877 offers an illustration of their mode of judgment: "Travellers and missionaries tell us that the same sweet airs which are so often heard in religious meetings in America, set to Christian hymns, are to be recognized in the boats and palm-roofed houses of Africa, set to heathen words and that the same wild stories of Buh Rabbit, Buh Wolf, and other *Buhs* that are so charming to the ears of American children, are to be heard to this day in Africa, differing only in drapery necessary to the change of scene."[5] Owens thus condemns not only black Americans, but also the continent of Africa, to a prelapsarian status. Joel Chandler Harris, who was encouraged by Owens to begin collecting black folktales, continued this impulse by making his Uncle Remus a childlike figure whose designated audience was white plantation children. Bernard Wolfe, a twentieth-century commentator, had the proslavery faction and its postbellum descendants in mind when he wrote: "Uncle Remus—a kind of blackface Will Rogers complete with standard minstrel dialect and plantation shuffle—has had remarkable staying power in our popular culture."[6] Wolfe might have added, and in our literary culture. Regardless of one's angle of vision, black Americans emerge from the foregoing reflections of the nineteenth-century white mind as childish, lesser members of the human family. Their creative efforts were judged accordingly.

Thus far I have dealt only with white spokesmen who cannot be called literary critics in any conventional sense. On the other hand, I have selected these commentators because I feel that their statements represent general American attitudes and pervasive white American patterns of judging black art that have influenced virtually every white American literary critic who has sought to analyze black American works of verbal art.

In the first literary history of America, for example, Moses Coit Tyler writes:

> The other prominent representative of the town of Boston in the poetry of this period [1763–1776] is Phillis Wheatly [*sic*], a gentle-minded and intelligent slave girl, whose name still survives among us in the shape of a tradition vaguely testifying to the existence of poetic talent in this particular member of the African race. Unfortunately, a glance at what she wrote

> will show that there is no adequate basis for such tradition, and that the significance of her career belongs rather to the domain of anthropology, or of hagiology, than to that of poetry—whether American or African. Her verses which were first published in a collected form in London in 1773, under the title, "Poems on Various Subjects, Religious and Moral," attracted for a time considerable curiosity, both in England and in America,—not at all, however, because the verses were good, but because they were written by one from whom even bad verses were too good to be expected.[7]

Tyler's comments include Wheatley among the representatives of a particular region, and his censure of the black writer follows a condemnation of all New England for its "poetic poverty." His indictment of Wheatley is, thus, predictable. There is a genuine ambivalence in the passage, however. Tyler is republican enough in *The Literary History of the American Revolution* to view slavery's abolition as a moral good, but he seems perplexed about the identity of the black "human brethren" who have been set free. His ironical tone—an almost whimsical detachment from a debate surrounding "African" creative ability—is double-edged. He seems, on the one hand, to deride a "tradition vaguely testifying" to black creative ability. On the other hand, he at least acknowledges this tradition as a reason for including the black poet among New England writers. He is certain, in short, that Wheatley's poems are valueless, but he is hesitant to ascribe exclusively racial reasons for their shortcomings. Assuredly, Africans are human, but Tyler is not prepared to answer for their creative ability. He is willing to assign this task to anthropologists who, in Tyler's era, studied "developing" races. The mention of hagiology, one suspects, is intended as a rebuff to those who lavished what Tyler considered excessive praise on Wheatley.

Certainly the author of *The Literary History* does not stand alone in his less than enthusiastic estimate of African creativity. White American critics from Barrett Wendell to the author of a recent *Saturday Review* article have always vacillated between a tendency to exclude blacks altogether from the world of art and an inclination to include them as infants of the spring.[8] At the turn of the century, both Wendell and his influential contemporary William Dean Howells expressed their views on black American creativity. A quotation from Wendell's *A Literary History of America* makes his stance abundantly clear: "However human, native Africans are still savage; and although, long before the Civil War, the Southern slaves had shown such sensitiveness to comparatively civilized conditions as to have lost their superficial savagery, and indeed as still to warrant, in many hopeful minds, even the franchise which was ultimately granted to them, the spectre of darkest Africa loomed behind them all."[9] This statement violently yokes together Jefferson's conclusions with the bitter dogmas of the proslavery faction.

Howells offers a contrasting contemporary opinion. He acknowledges that the dialect verse of Paul Laurence Dunbar and also the stories included in Charles Chesnutt's *The Conjure Woman* are superb works of art because they capture the pathos, humor, and inherent limitations of black Americans. For Howells, a sanguine philosophy of life and a positive evaluation of optimistic works of art were wedded. While his critiques were often beneficial to black artists, therefore, they were sometimes disastrous. Dunbar's poems in standard literary English—many of which are extremely pessimistic—receive only passing notice. And Chesnutt's telling novel of southern racial injustice earns the following comment: "The book [*The Marrow of Tradition*] is, in fact, bitter, bitter. There is no reason in history why it should not be so, if wrong is to be repaid with hate, and yet it would be better if it were not so bitter."[10] Believing that truth could spring only from the "large cheerful average of health and success and happy life," Howells hardly expected black Americans to lament or turn bitter. Morality, for him, penetrated all things, and if blacks (whose range of existence spanned "appetite and emotion")[11] could not reflect his point of view, then something was clearly awry in their human makeup. So the man whom Mark Twain described as like himself—an old derelict—floated on in the strange seas of a complex and turbulently racist era.

The twentieth century has, for the most part, offered white American responses in harmony with those already detailed. The New Critics, for example, when on occasion they evaluated black creativity, generally concluded like Jefferson that it "escapes incessantly from every restraint of reason and taste." David Littlejohn's *Black on White: A Critical Survey of Writing by American Negroes* is a recent, arch example of the New Critical perspective on black creativity. Politically progressive white critics (usually Marxists or Marxist-Leninists) have frequently followed the pattern of the abolitionists. Realizing the necessity for a black advance guard if meaningful American social change is to occur, such critics have enlisted blacks under their banners. Like their nineteenth-century prototypes, however, they have been stung to fierce retorts when black spokesmen have become energetic in their own behalf. Irving Howe's treatment of *Native Son* offers a case in point. In "Black Boys and Native Sons," Howe sees Wright as a paradigm for the creativity of black America. Ralph Ellison and James Baldwin, by comparison, have, according to the progressive white critic, worshiped false gods. Howe's article "At Ease with Apocalypse," however, reveals an altered perspective. Here *Native Son* is labeled a "crude" book. (One almost hears the cry, "There is roguery somewhere!") When it became apparent to Howe (from the quick, brilliant responses of Ellison) that blacks would not suffer his prescriptive, political formulas, he turned against even his model black artist.

There have also been some twentieth-century white writers whose criticisms read like the efforts of the proslavery adherents. A commentator like John H. Nelson, for example, could set forth a list of black American characteristics like the following: "irrepressible spirits," "complete absorption in the present moment," "whimsicality," "irresponsibility," "intense superstition," "freedom from resentment."[12] Defined in this manner, the black writer is expected to provide easy, exotic fare for an audience composed of white children.

The origins of white America's traditional responses to black creativity may be obscured by endless pages of interpretation. Behind these apologies, however, lie fundamental attitudes and patterns of judgment that have governed a felt rejection of black American art and culture. W. E. B. Du Bois speaks of that "other world which does not know and does not want to know our power." There is another dimension: a world ordered by limiting codes of evaluation and, hence, incapable of knowing the black spokesman's expressive power. Van Wyck Brooks divides American literature into three categories: highbrow, lowbrow, and middlebrow. Analogically, one might view white America's judgments of black creativity as encompassing three basic patterns: exclusion, qualified acceptance, and an amused contempt for the supposed infantile character of black life and art. Because so many white spokesmen have worked within this limiting range, they have seldom granted to black creativity the kind of loud, unequivocal praise that they have lavished on white works of art.

But if black creativity is the result of a context—of webs of meaning—different in kind and degree from those conceived within the narrow attitudinal categories of white America, it seems possible that the semantic force of black creativity might escape the white critic altogether. And where black American works of literature and verbal art are involved, a case can certainly be made for the cultural specificity of meaning. The argument involved, however, requires an open, analytical mind on the part of both the investigator and his audience. But it is worth pursuing if one is interested in comprehending not only the expressive manifestations of black America, but also some additional reasons for the white commentator's ofttimes superficial accounts of black verbal art.

7 *Toward a Critical Prospect for the Future*

A crucial factor in the type of argument I would like to propose is the peculiar relationship of Africa to the English language. Coming into English in a trading situation, making contact with Indo-European languages through their contact with adventurers in search of wealth, native Africans moved toward a pidgin English.[1] This language comprised vocabulary items from various European languages. It was a complex natural language, possessing its own grammatical rules. But these grammatical rules are not the most significant factor for this discussion. The social and psychological situation of Africans and their vocabulary borrowings offer more interesting speculations. As they witnessed whites destroying their internal trade (both slave and other), viewed the introduction of firearms, saw Europeans struggling ruthlessly for commercial advantage, and felt themselves driven from stable systems of social organization to enslavement in a vast pattern of trade that claimed millions of lives, what conjunctions existed for black Africans at the very outset—during that extended pre-English instant—before the adoption of English lexical items?

One can assume that words like *white, slave, freedom* and a variety of others had a significance for African borrowers that was firmly rooted in their complex relationship to the trans-Atlantic slave trade. Since the situation and values of Africans were substantially different from those of white Europeans, the pidgin English of African (and later, of course, black American) speakers must have carried meanings (semantic levels of the lexicon) quite different from those held by Europeans. But because the second language had been adopted or learned for purposes of trade, the vocabulary of the two groups would have been almost identical. In the public intercourse between Europeans and Africans, in other words, the speaking situation, or the communicative context, itself would have determined certain meanings.

Recognizing the irony/absurdity of the disjunctions between the words (concepts) they were adopting and their own native concepts, as well as the disparity between the European's gift of civilization and the realities of the slave trade, Africans would scarcely have adopted in toto the meanings of their European exploiters. Language (Edward Sapir to the contrary notwithstanding)[2] is not an invisible garment that drapes itself about the human spirit, lending a predetermined form to all symbolic expression. Africans were not completely bound, in other words, by the categories of European languages. They could engage, at will, in a process of semantic inversion.

Ludwig Wittgenstein accounted for the possibility of such linguistic behavior in his *Philosophical Investigations.* Even though Wittgenstein believed that language usage—the speaking situation or language game—governed meanings and gave coherence to human cultures, he also knew that human beings are never trapped in a hopeless continuum of language games. *Freedom* can become *not freedom.* Negation—even repudiation—is a human possibility.[3] Langston Hughes offers a poetical example:

> There are words like *Freedom*
> Sweet and wonderful to say.
> On my heartstrings freedom sings
> All day everyday.

> There are words like *Liberty*
> That almost make me cry.
> If you had known what I know
> You would know why.[4]

The investigator of black American literature can start, therefore, from the answer Wittgenstein provides for his hypothetical questioner in the *Philosophical Investigations:*

> "But doesn't what you say come to this: that there is no pain, for example, without pain-behavior?"—It comes to this, only of a living human being can one say: it has sensations; it sees; is blind; hears; is deaf; is conscious or unconscious.

If blacks "entered" the English language with values and concepts antithetical to those of the white externality surrounding them, then their vocabulary is less important than the underlying codes, or semantic fields, that governed meaning. What I am suggesting is the possibility that whites—moving exclusively within the boundaries of their own semantic categories—have taken the words of the black work of verbal art at face value, or worse, at a value assigned by their own limiting attitudes and patterns of judgment.

Two brief examples serve to clarify. The first is offered by Charles Chesnutt's *The Conjure Woman*. Published as a volume in 1899, the work seemed guaranteed of success by the white critical acclaim that had earlier greeted one of its stories. "The Goophered Grapevine" had been praised by white readers when it appeared in an 1896 issue of the *Atlantic*. Few readers were aware of Chesnutt's race, and in the heyday of the Plantation School, who could expect a black spokesman to go against the weave of what Oscar Handlin calls the "Linnaean Web."[5] Chesnutt's short story seemed simply another effort in a long line of works dedicated to a portrait of blacks as amiable, childlike creatures devoted to strumming and humming all day on the old plantation. Howells and other white critics lauded the story on this assumption.

There is no absence of linguistic clues to a quite different set of expectations where the collection of stories is concerned, however. In fact, the title of Chesnutt's book reveals his deeper intentions and signals the authentic array of conditions that govern an appropriate reading of the text. The protagonist—the moving force behind the action of each of *The Conjure Woman*'s stories—is the black conjurer, and as the black historian John Blassingame writes:

> In addition to these activities [religious and recreational], several other customs prevented the slaves from identifying with the ideals of their masters. Because of their superstitions and beliefs in fortune tellers, witches, magic and conjurers, many of the slaves constructed a psychological defense against total dependence on and submission to their masters. Whatever his power, the master was a puny man compared to the supernatural. Often the most powerful and significant individual on the plantation was the conjurer.[6]

Blassingame goes on to point out that by shrewdness and an industrious countermanding of the slave system the conjurer gained control over blacks and whites alike.

Such a conclusion, of course, cannot be inferred from the collection's title alone. It does indicate, however, that white critics unaware of the meaning that the conjurer held for black Americans were ill-prepared to evaluate Chesnutt's stories. The referents for such critics would have resided totally outside the lexical and conceptual fields that assured autonomy and a unique sense of the black self for Chesnutt and for his selected black readers.

The argument here is not unlike the one adduced in an earlier chapter to explain the distinctiveness in concept and value of Wheatley's verse and Vassa's narrative. If, however, my invocation of Chesnutt seems an example of "justification by the little-known text," one can turn to a more celebrated work—Richard Wright's *Native Son.* Having already set forth an analysis of the black folk concepts and strategies that I feel give semantic force to the novel,[7] I wish to look for a moment at James Emanuel's analysis of linguistic metaphors in Wright's text.[8] Insisting that *Native Son* is rooted in a sui generis experience, Emanuel points out a host of recurrent language structures that mark Bigger Thomas's fictive development. Images of crucifixion, confinement, claustrophobia, heat, and light all speak of the black protagonist's imprisonment by a white world oblivious to his humanity. The novel's rhetorical structures carry one, finally, to the folk level of black American culture, to the "forms of things unknown." Taking the words *furnace, flight, snow, curtain,* and so on at their face value, however, many white critics have failed to add to our understanding of Wright's creativity.

Thus far in analyzing black American literature and culture I have talked only of the semanticity of the word. However, while this consideration is primary, it is but a part of a larger perspective that emphasizes what Professor Elizabeth Traugott designates as "the attitudes fostered by linguistics" in literary critical investigations.[9] Traugott uses the phrase to specify the governing assumption on the part of literary analysts that the methods and models of linguistics and the linguistic investigation of texts can yield significant results when applied to a culture and its verbal art. I have attempted to demonstrate in previous chapters the kinds of concerns that are raised by an attention to the language of black America and its literary works of art. What is ultimately involved, however, is the entire history—the full discourse—that constitutes black American culture.

A final example serves to clarify. A rigorous analysis of the language in chapter eleven of Ellison's *Invisible Man*—the factory hospital episode—reveals a fundamental opposition between two ways of life, two conceptions of human nature. Man at play (*Homo ludens*) stands at one pole, while man at work (*Homo laborans*) stands at the other. The entire chapter (and, indeed, the whole of *Invisible Man*) can be analyzed in terms of this binary relationship.[10]

The chapter begins when a nurse asks the protagonist: "What is your name?" There is a pause, and then the opening triad from Beethoven's Fifth Symphony sounds in the mind of the protagonist. We have a naming ceremony introduced by the opening notes of the most well known, romantic work in the symphonic repertoire. Beethoven shades immediately into the awesome hum of a machine.

Rather than counterpoint, there is transition: man's epic, romantic spirit is transformed into mechanical energy. For the protagonist, who is bound among the nodes of the machine, the results of this transformation are painful. But when he loses consciousness, Beethoven's and the machine's force fades into an agrarian reverie that is characterized by a "Sunday air" entitled "The Holy City." The song is played by a band which, as the text unfolds, appears increasingly regimented and is finally engulfed by a swarm of white gnats: "the dark trumpeter breathed them in and expelled them through the bell of his golden horn, a live white cloud mixing with tones upon the torpid air." Returning to consciousness, the narrator poses mental questions to his captors:

> Oh, doctor, I thought drowsily, did you ever wade in a brook before breakfast? Ever chew on sugar cane? You know, doc, the same fall day I first saw the hounds chasing black men in stripes and chains my grandmother sat with me and sang with twinkling eyes:
>
> "Godamighty made a monkey
> Godamighty made a whale
> And Godamighty made a 'gator
> With hickeys all over his tail . . ."

With this brief summary of the episode completed, let me return to the binary relationship postulated above. *Homo laborans*, technological man, seeks the power to organize and control the collective labor needed for industry. Like the rulers of the early irrigation civilizations, he perceives man not as an end in himself, but as a means to an end, a unit of production.[11] The spiritual is subservient to the mechanical for *Homo laborans*—the emotional gives way to technological rationalism. In chapter eleven, the characters who array themselves around *Homo laborans* are the nurses and doctors, old Friendly Face (appearing in the somber garb of a Puritan divine), the scholar, and, preeminently, the Directoi. The factory is an icon of man as tool-user, as technocrat or maker.

Man at play, by contrast, is man as a symbolic animal, a "speaking subject." If the ambit of technological man is control and power, the orbit of man at play is freedom.[12] The most striking representation of *Homo ludens'* opposition to enslaving labor is offered by the black convicts fleeing from the chain gang. The event is represented as occurring on the same day that the narrator's grandmother sang a folksong whose cosmology—like that of the song played by the band—begins not with man on earth, but with God in heaven. The opposition between the secular and the spiritual is profound. *Homo ludens* is, ultimately, incapable of communicating with those governed by a limiting conception of man as laborer: "A terrible sense of loneliness came over me; they seemed to enact a mysterious pantomime . . . . Other faces came up, their mouths working with *soundless* fury. But we are all human, I thought, wondering what I meant" (italics mine). What the "I" means, it seems to me, is that the very nature of the concept "human" is in the process of definition. Finally, *Homo ludens* is what anthropologists call a "liminal" character,[13] a marginal figure like the shaman, or the active tradition bearers in cultural rites of reversal. He is representative of what Ellison calls "the mysterious, underground aspect of human personality." The world is upside down—the women are dressed as men, those at the bottom have assumed control, the royal household is subject to parody, and the outrageous trickster has won the victory.[14] The narrator reports on his own discovery, "I laughed, deep, deep inside me, giddy with the delight of self-discovery and the desire to hide it. Somehow *I* was Buckeye the Rabbit."

The factory hospital designed to make a "new man" of the narrator gives birth to the playful, ironic, dozens-quipping trickster whose name is "freedom," whose name is "human." There is an air of slow revelation about the entire chapter, and the words *hidden* and *mystery* recur. *Homo ludens* is hidden at the margins and is yet to be discovered by the technological "detectives." The expectation of those who control the society's machinery is characterized by their refusal to explore the margins. And it is in this region that *Homo ludens* plays and has his being.

My hypothesis—for this example is obviously abbreviated—is that the opposition that gives meaning to the factory hospital episode can be viewed as fundamental for the textual structure of *Invisible Man* as a whole. There is a suggestion of this in the narrator's questions to the Director. He asks if the Director knows Messrs. Norton, Emerson, and Bledsoe—all characters grouped around *Homo laborans.* He further emphasizes his ludic, self-governing nature when he refuses to accept the bridge as a means of progress at the end of the chapter. Instead, he plunges into the earth. He takes the subway, the hidden underground. And there he finds, seated across the aisle, a "young platinum blonde" nibbling a delicious apple. The woman who is traditionally invested in America with white, technological, man's morality—the new Eve—is below, awaiting the ironically black and liminal Adam.

Although I suggest that the whole of *Invisible Man* can be understood in terms of the patterning of the factory hospital episode, I do not want to claim there is a single, irreducible formula that "explains" the novel. Surely, there are other oppositions as important as the one discussed here. But since *Invisible Man's* various chapters take up the same motifs time and again,[15] it seems useful to seek out the generative relationships that give coherence to these motifs. The Battle Royal chapter, the Trueblood encounter, the Liberty Paints episode with Lucius Brockway and the boilers, and the whole of The Brotherhood section can be fruitfully analyzed in terms of the binary relationship that governs the factory hospital chapter. Only a close scrutiny of Ellison's language—almost a reading of the chapter's words as though they were opaque signs of a poetic discourse—enables one to hazard this conclusion.

What one is forced to hypothesize at the outset of an analysis of black creativity is *structure.* One must assume that beyond the surface of the individual words in Ellison's chapter there are complex ordering principles that make possible relationships like the one discussed here. I think one can discover such principles and their dependent structural relations only through an analysis of linguistic textual regularities that are deemed significant within a particular cultural context. The words selected for Ellison's chapter and their various combinations are grounded in a specific cultural history that has seen blacks continuously exploited as laborers and excluded from the ownership or direction of American means (whether land or technology) of production. Given Ellison's monumental brilliance, these basic conditions of the black situation are, not surprisingly, represented in *Invisible Man*.

The search for structural relationships in any literary text, I think, entails a knowledge of the full cultural discourse that provides a context. Man at work and man at play as they appear in *Invisible Man* could hardly constitute a salient opposition in a culture that had never come into contact with an extensive modern technology. Furthermore, if the trickster is not a seminal hero in a culture, one would scarcely expect this folk figure to play the key role assigned to "Buckeye the Rabbit" in the factory hospital episode. Finally, the literary investigator's attention is arrested by words such as *grandmother*, *folksong*, and *human* only if he or she is aware of black American concerns like the role of the matriarch in black and African cultures, the importance of music as an agency of instruction (and subversion) in black culture, and the omnipresent concern with ontology that has marked black intellectual history.

No analyst can understand the black literary text who is not conscious of the semantic levels of black culture. The journey to this level is by way of the whole discourse comprising black American culture. White American critics have repeatedly assumed prerogatives like those Ellison assigns to *Homo laborans*. Seeking to control, sum up, or categorize the black world in phrases drawn from their own peculiar cultural discourse, they have seldom learned how to converse with the natives of black American culture. In this sense, they have failed to enlarge the American universe of discourse.

Black American critics, on the other hand, have been compelled to conclusions like those implicit in the title of one of Michael Harper's volumes of poetry. "History is your own heartbeat," writes Harper, and he could have added that history is also the sound of your own voice returning through the discourse of your culture.[16] As a participant in black America's history and discourse, the black critic is a culture bearer. He is one who helps to spin the culture's webs of meaning. This does not automatically invest him with authority. But it does augur well for his chances of providing a "thick description" of black American literature and culture based on informed analyses of works of verbal art that he both perceives, and half creates.

Conclusion

I suggested at the beginning of this volume that the anthropology of art offers a general theory of art and culture that scholars of black American literature and culture might find useful in their work. My discussions in the preceding chapters have been in accord with a basic postulate of this theory: i.e., works of art must be studied by applying methods and models drawn from a number of intellectual disciplines. To analyze a culture's art from an anthropological perspective is, by necessity, to engage in an interdisciplinary enterprise. As the "science of man," anthropology provides an area where various social and behavioral sciences join forces to give birth to full and informative accounts (ethnographies) of human cultures. Guiding these interdisciplinary activities is the assumption that cultures are holistic organizations of life in which rule-governed systems (e.g., religion, politics, language, economics, kinship, and so on) operate in strategically interrelated ways. Insights into the operations of one cultural system may thus serve useful ends in the analysis of other systems.

In the foregoing chapters, I have employed methods and findings from the broad areas of linguistics and the linguistic investigation of texts in order to elucidate aspects of black

American culture such as its unique semantic fields, foregroundings, autobiographical acts, and functional oppositions. My analyses of these linguistic forms reveal governing principles, processes, and relationships of the black American cultural discourse as a whole. And they lead to my conclusion that a critical prospect for the future must be grounded in a general theory of art and culture like the anthropology of art. The theory, in turn, must be served by a methodology designed to explore language as a system that offers keys to the detailed understanding of human art and culture. Black Americans, as St. Clair Drake notes, have left the "legacy of their words" as one means of comprehending their sometimes anguished quest for terms for order.[1] It is only when we subject this legacy to appropriate analysis, however, that it yields its stores of meaning and allows us to make the journey back. One virtue of bringing to bear a general theory of art and culture in the critical process is that it makes available sound hypotheses, fruitful interpretive strategies, and rigorous standards of analysis, yielding insights on the art and style that characterize a unique culture in America. The benefits that accrue to the theory from analyses of black American literature and culture include the provision of additional data to expand the explanatory range of the anthropology of art. The reciprocity implied here is a sanguine prospect, and it is tempting to think of concluding with its optimistic forecast. It would be less than honest, however, to close without sharing a stretch of discourse by Chinua Achebe that has haunted my imagination since the commencement of this project. For I am certain that my decision to focus on language and linguistics in the present volume was motivated by premises like those implied in the following observation:

> we know that language is not inherent in man—the capacity for language; but not language. Therefore there must have been a time in the very distant past when our ancestors did not have it. Let us imagine a very simple incident in those days. A man strays into a rock shelter without knowing that another is there finishing a meal in the dark interior. The first hint our newcomer gets of this fact is a loose rock hurled at his

> head. In a different kind of situation, which we shall call . . . *human,* that confrontation might have been resolved less destructively by the simple question: *What do you want?* or even an angry *Get out of here*![2]

The literary texts of black America provide clear evidence that blacks have attempted to order the disruption and chaos occasioned by their confrontation with the West through language—and not always with stones tossed at the heads of their oppressors. One takes up such verbal structures in order to make known the range and significance of a singular journey. Even the most rudimentary facts of our existence as articulate tradition bearers have been discounted in the past. There is no justification for their continued neglect in what promises to be a more informed future. My search for analytical means of contributing to such a future is motivated by the compelling necessity to make known black America's heroic acts of language and its attempts to humanize an ofttimes brutal and dehumanizing existence through the power of the word.

Notes

INTRODUCTION

1. One of the more detailed and suggestive studies of linguistic discourse is M. A. K. Halliday and Ruquaiya Hasan's *Cohesion in English* (London: Longman, 1976). Zellig Harris's "Discourse Analysis," (*Language* 28 [1952]: 1–30) is a frequently cited work as well. Clyde Kluckohn offers a statement that lends force to my analogy in his essay "Cultural Anthropology: New Uses for 'Barbarians,'" in Lynn White, Jr., ed., *Frontiers of Knowledge in the Study of Man* (New York: Harper, 1956): "Since language exemplifies the cultural process in such a pure form, many anthropologists use language as a theoretical model for the study of culture generally. It is also in the field of anthropological linguistics that the most rigorous methods have been developed and where the frontiers of cultural anthropology are being swept back the most dramatically" (pp. 41–42). The work on language and culture of Franz Boas, Edward Sapir, Benjamin Lee Whorf, Leslie White, and others laid the groundwork for Kluckohn's assertion.

2. Though I sincerely wish it were my own, the analogy is a traditional one. Ludwig Wittgenstein employs various cultural "games" in his *Philosophical Investigations* to clarify his observations on "language games," i.e., the rule-governed verbal behaviors of men and women in society. My use of a game of chess derives from the work of another philosopher of language, John R. Searle's *Speech Acts: An Essay in the Philosophy of Language* (Cambridge: Cambridge University Press, 1969).

3. "Thick Description: Toward an Interpretive Theory of Culture," in *The Interpretation of Cultures* (New York: Basic, 1973), pp. 3–30. The following discussion of Geertz proceeds in terms of this essay.

4. *Culture and Communication* (Cambridge: University Press, 1976), p. 69.

5. The field is symbolic anthropology. Geertz is a major scholar in the field, and so, too, is Victor Turner. For a thorough introduction, one might consult Janet L. Dolgin, David S. Kemnitzer, and David M. Schneider, eds., *Symbolic Anthropology* (New York: Columbia University Press, 1977). The reader might also wish to consult Barbara A. Babcock, ed., *The Reversible World: Symbolic Inversion in Art and Society* (Ithaca: Cornell University Press, 1978). For a brief, but classic, view of Turner's work, see *International Encyclopedia of the Social Sciences,* s.v. "Myth and Symbol."

6. To gain some idea of the extensiveness of the scholarship, the reader can survey Robert Scholes's bibliographical appendix in *Structuralism in Literature* (New Haven: Yale University Press, 1974). He can also consult Terence Hawkes's bibliography in *Structuralism and Semiotics* (Berkeley and Los Angeles: University of California Press, 1977). Jonathan Culler's twenty-one page, fine-print bibliography in *Structuralist Poetics* (Ithaca: Cornell University Press, 1975) provides a further illustration of the scholarly interest the twentieth century has shown in linguistic investigations of literature.

7. See Stanley Fish's "Literature in the Reader: Affective Stylistics," in *Self-Consuming Artifacts* (Berkeley: University of California Press, 1972), pp. 384–427. See also Wolfgang Iser's "The Reading Process: A Phenomenological Approach," in Ralph Cohen, ed., *New Directions in Literary History* (Baltimore: Johns Hopkins University Press, 1973), pp. 125–45. There is also the work in psycholinguistics of Roger Brown and of Herbert and Eve Clark, and Hunter Diack's *Reading and the Psychology of Perceptions* (Greenwood, N.Y.: Greenwood, 1972). George L. Dillon's *Language Processing and the Reading of Literature* (Bloomington: Indiana University Press, 1978) has been recently released.

8. I have taken the term itself from Leonard B. Meyer's perceptive discussion, "Forgery and the Anthropology of Art," in *Music, the Arts, and Ideas* (Chicago: University of Chicago Press, 1967).

9. "And Shine Swam On," in LeRoi Jones and Larry Neal, eds., *Black Fire: An Anthology of Afro-American Writing* (New York: Morrow, 1968), pp. 638–56.

10. The sense of African art "in motion" that Neal is calling for can be seen as a function of the general case for instructive, educational arrangements of anthropological museums stated by J. Aldon Mason almost twenty years ago: "Life-sized groups, dioramas, and miniature groups give a visual impression that can be achieved by no other means.... Objects should ordinarily be shown in their natural milieu and except in special and temporary exhibitions of primitive art, not shown as objects of art" ("Observations on the Function of Museums in Anthropology," in *Culture in History:*

Essays in Honor of Paul Radin, ed. Stanley Diamond [New York: Columbia University Press, 1960], p. 341). The Yale art historian Robert F. Thompson's consultation produced a striking modern instance of this concept in the National Gallery of Art's "African Art and Motion" exhibit of 1974.

CHAPTER ONE

1. *Terms For Order,* ed. Stanley Hyman and Barbara Karmiller (Bloomington: Indiana University Press, 1964). What I intend by the phrase is a subtle combination, not only rhetorical or linguistic strategies for confronting life, but also philosophical constructs and plans of action. Another way of stating the object would be: an appropriate world view, appropriately articulated.

2. "The Function of a Criticism of Black American Literature," MS., First Annual Spring Symposium, Afro-American Studies Programs, University of Pennsylvania, 1975.

3. *The Life of Olaudah Equiano or Gustavus Vassa the African Written by Himself,* in Arna Bontemps, ed., *Great Slave Narratives* (Boston: Beacon, 1969), p. 27.

4. Melville J. Herskovits, *The Myth of a Negro Past* (Boston: Beacon, 1958); W. E. B. Du Bois, *The Souls of Black Folk,* in John Hope Franklin, ed., *Three Negro Classics* (New York: Avon, 1965). See also Du Bois's *The Negro* and *The Gift of Black Folk* and Herskovits's *American Negro*.

5. See E. Franklin Frazier, *The Negro in the United States* (New York: Macmillan, 1957) and Stanley Elkins, *Slavery* (Chicago: University of Chicago Press, 1976). See also Frazier's *The Negro Church in America*.

6. John W. Blassingame, *The Slave Community* (New York: Oxford University Press, 1973); Paul Carter Harrison, *The Drama of Nommo: Black Theater in the African Continuum* (New York: Grove, 1973); William D. Piersen, "Puttin' Down Ole Massa: African Satire in the New World," in Daniel J. Crowley, ed., *African Folklore in the New World* (Austin: University of Texas Press, 1977).

7. *Jupiter Hammon, American Negro Poet: Selections from His Writings and a Bibliography,* ed. Oscar Wegelin (Miami: Mnemosyne, 1969), p. 26.

8. In Dorothy Porter, ed., *Early Negro Writing 1760–1837* (Boston: Beacon, 1971), p. 315.

9. *Jupiter Hammon,* p. 32.

10. Ibid., p. 30.

11. Ibid., p. 42.

12. *Memoir and Poems of Phillis Wheatley* (Boston: Light and Horton, 1835), pp. 9–10. This is a standard biographical source for Wheatley. I have drawn many of the details of my subsequent comments from its pages.

13. From Thomas Jefferson, *Notes on the State of Virginia*, ed. William Peden (Chapel Hill: University of North Carolina Press, 1954), p. 140.

14. *Phillis Wheatley in the Black American Beginnings* (Detroit: Broadside, 1975).

15. For a view of the controversy, see Merle Richmond, *Bid the Vassal Soar* (Washington, D.C.: Howard University Press, 1974). See also Sidney Kaplan, *The Black Presence in the Era of the American Revolution* (New York: New York Graphic Society, 1973).

16. *The Negro Author in America* (New York: Columbia University Press, 1931), p. 16. Loggins's work offers an account of the "development" of the black writer in America from 1760 to 1900. It still affords one of the most complete surveys of early black writing in America. Arthur P. Davis's *From the Dark Tower* (Washington, D.C.: Howard University Press, 1974) has the stated goal of complementing Loggins's work. It continues the story from 1900 to the present.

17. LeRoi Jones, *Home: Social Essays* (New York: Morrow, 1972), p. 285.

18. Robinson, *Phillis Wheatley*, p. 14.

19. Ibid., p. 15.

20. "Christian Calling," in Perry Miller and Thomas H. Johnson, eds., *The Puritans* (New York: American Books, 1938), p. 319.

21. In *The Poems of Phillis Wheatley*, ed. Julian D. Mason (Chapel Hill: University of North Carolina Press, 1966), pp. 5–6.

22. Umberto Eco, *A Theory of Semiotics* (Bloomington: Indiana University Press, 1976).

23. *White Man, Listen!* (Garden City, N.Y.: Anchor, 1964), p. 75. Wright states a polarity: the black American literary tradition can, in his view, be divided into "entity" and "identity." Those writers who wrote with a sense that they were part of the general culture illustrate entity. Those who felt they had to work against great odds to overcome a sense of alienation demonstrate the pole of identity. Beyond this spectrum lie what Wright calls the "forms of things unknown," i.e., black folk expression.

24. Kaplan, *Black Presence*, p. 157.

25. "'This Bread I Break'—Language and Interpretation," *A Review of English Literature* 6 (1965): 66–75. For a detailed account of Russian formalist contributions to the investigation of narrative texts, the reader should consult Scholes, *Structuralism in Literature*, pp. 74–91.

26. "I was baptized in St. Margaret's Church, Westminster, in February 1759, by my present name . . . I was sometimes . . . with my master at his rendezvous house, which was at the foot of Westminster bridge. Here I used to enjoy myself in playing about the bridge stairs, and often in the waterman's wherries, with other boys." As he is playing in a wherry one day, two "stout boys"

demand that he disembark and enter another boat. "Just as I got one of my feet into the other boat, the boys shoved it off, so that I fell into the Thames; and, not being able to swim, I should unavoidably have been drowned, but for the assistance of some watermen who providentially came to my relief" (*Life*, p. 49). One way of coding this is that the waters of Christian baptism and those of the English Thames converge. Is the result of Vassa's conversion in an alien land a blessing or a threatened cultural extinction? There is ample ground for speculation.

27. See note 8 above.

28. Following Eco's procedure, slashes indicate an expression unit, guillemets a *sememe*, or a segmentation in the content-plane.

29. *Semantics*, vol. 1, (Cambridge: Cambridge University Press, 1977), p. 254.

30. Here I am invoking a structuralist prospect best illustrated in the works of Claude Lévi-Strauss. One of Lévi-Strauss's responses to a fellow participant at a Wenner-Gren conference in the 1950s serves to clarify the point of view. Having briefly discussed the structural relationships in certain myths, the French anthropologist was congratulated for recognizing that myths were products of man's reaction to the natural world. Lévi-Strauss answered: "I do not admit that myths are about symbols of nature. It just happened that, dealing with origin myths, I referred to natural elements. But it would have been equally possible to describe these myths by using ritual operations, kinship behavior, etc. The nature of the elements is irrelevant to the structure of the myth; what is important is how certain things are correlated, not what these things are. They may well be anything" (Sol Tax et al., eds., *An Appraisal of Anthropology Today* [Chicago: University of Chicago Press, 1953], p. 332). Another way of stating the point of view is that of Merleau-Ponty: "We have always to do only with sign structures whose meanings, being nothing other than the way in which signs behave toward one another and are distinguished from one another, cannot be set forth independently of them" (*Signs* [Evanston, Ill.: Northwestern University Press, 1964], p. 42).

31. From "Straight Seeking," in Andrew Salkey, ed., *Breaklight: The Poetry of the Caribbean* (New York: Doubleday, 1973).

32. From "To the Humane and Benevolent Inhabitants of the City and County of Philadelphia, Address Delivered August 10, 1817," in Porter, ed., *Early Negro Writing*, p. 265.

33. "A decade of anticolonization agitation gave free Negroes of the North a sense of community. Out of this agitation came the pioneer Negro abolitionists, the Negro convention movement and the first Negro newspaper, *Freedom's Journal*, which was published for the first time on March 16, 1827, by Samuel E. Cornish, a Presbyterian minister, and John B. Russwurm, the first Negro college

graduate (Bowdoin, 1826). Richard Allen, the great AME bishop, was the leader of the first Negro convention which met in Philadelphia in 1830, three years before the founding of the American Anti-Slavery Society" (Lerone Bennett, Jr., *Before the Mayflower* [Baltimore: Penguin, 1968], p. 131).

34. Porter, ed., *Early Negro Writing,* p. 266.

35. Ibid., pp. 266–67.

36. Ibid., p. 266.

37. For a view of this tradition, see Jean Fagin Yellin's *The Intricate Knot* (New York: New York University Press, 1972). Prominent white writers of the Plantation School included John Pendleton Kennedy, William Gilmore Simms, and James Kirke Paulding. All three were devoted to a conception of the southern plantation as the dwelling place of aristocratic whites who traced their lineage to European royalty and fractious and comic blacks who followed theirs to a seamy African abyss. Addison Gayle, Jr., has something to say about such views in "Cultural Strangulation: Black Literature and the White Aesthetic," in Addison Gayle, Jr., ed., *The Black Aesthetic* (New York: Doubleday, 1971), pp. 39–46.

CHAPTER TWO

1. *Autobiographical Acts* (Baltimore: Johns Hopkins University Press, 1976). "All reading (or writing) involves us in choice: we choose to pursue a style or subject matter, to struggle with or against a design. We also choose, as passive as it may seem, to take part in an interaction, and it is here that generic labels have their use. The genre does not tell us the style or construction of a text as much as how we should expect to 'take' that style or mode of construction—what force it should have for us" (p. 4). Professor Bruss is drawing on speech-act theory as delineated by J. L. Austin, Paul Strawson, and John Searle. The nature, or force, of the speech act combines context, conditions, and intentions; it is called by the philosophers of language mentioned above the *illocutionary force* of an utterance. If the illocutionary force of a speech act is one involving certain rules, contexts, and intentions of self-revelation, the act can be called autobiographical. What I shall be investigating in the next few pages is the peculiar illocutionary force of certain black autobiographies produced during the nineteenth century. For an account of black autobiography, see Stephen Butterfield, *Black Autobiography in America* (Amherst: University of Massachusetts Press, 1974).

2. Rebecca Chalmers Barton, *Witnesses for Freedom* (New York: Harper, 1948), p. xii.

3. George McMichael, ed., *Anthology of American Literature* (New York: Macmillan, 1974), 1:228.

4. *The Examined Self* (Princeton: Princeton University Press, 1964), p. 39.

5. *A Short History of Existentialism* (New York: Philosophical Library, 1949), p. 31. See also Jean Wahl, *Philosophies of Existence: An Introduction to the Basic Thought of Kierkegaard, Heidegger, Jaspers, Marcel, Sartre* (New York: Schocken, 1959).

6. *The Ideological Origins of Black Nationalism* (Boston: Beacon, 1972).

7. *Narrative of the Life of Frederick Douglass an American Slave Written by Himself* (New York: Signet, 1968), p. 21.

8. In a fine analysis of the *Narrative* ("Animal Farm Unbound," *New Letters* 43 [1977]: 25–48), H. Bruce Franklin explores the significance for American literature of white assumptions that blacks are outside the human family. But cf. my own treatment of animal imagery in Douglass, which appeared in my collection of essays *Long Black Song* (Charlottesville: University Press of Virginia, 1972); and Albert Stone, "Identity and Art in Frederick Douglass' Narrative," *CLA Journal* 17 (1973): 192–213.

9. Quoted from Janheinz Jahn, *Neo-African Literature* (New York: Grove, 1969), p. 240.

10. *The Life and Times of Frederick Douglass Written by Himself* (New York: Collier, 1973), p. 442.

11. *Witnesses for Freedom*, pp. 3–40.

12. John Blassingame, "Black Autobiographies as History and Literature," *Black Scholar* 5 (1973–74): 2–9.

13. *Up from Slavery*, in Franklin, ed., *Three Negro Classics*, p. 107. Unless otherwise specified, all citations refer to this edition.

14. The concept of "fictive discourse" is drawn from the work of Barbara Herrnstein Smith. Professor Smith makes a distinction between "natural discourse" and fictive discourse. While "a natural utterance is an historical *event* [and] like any other event, it occupies a specific and unique point in time and space," a fictive utterance is historically indeterminate. It is possible, therefore, for it to postulate and explore propositions that are considered "timeless." Works of imaginative literature, that is to say, may be thought of as discourse structures that imply analytical propositions. An analytical proposition, according to philosophy, is one of the conditions of possibility of reason. All men of reason understand that "If X then Y." The truth-value of such propositions is not contingent upon empirical reference, but upon reason, operating in a timeless dimension. See "Poetry as Fiction," in Cohen, ed., *New Directions in Literary History*, pp. 165–87. See also her book *On the Margins of Discourse* (Chicago: University of Chicago Press, 1978). For a discussion of analytic propositions in relation to speech acts, see Searle, *Speech Acts*.

15. The discussion here is based on C. S. Hall and Gardner Lindzey, *Theories of Personality* (New York: Wiley, 1978), pp. 160–61.

16. Ibid., p. 161.

17. Bruss, in stating her rules, or appropriateness conditions, for autobiographical acts of discourse says: "(a) under existing conventions, a claim is made for the truth-value of what the autobiography reports—no matter how difficult that truth-value might be to ascertain, whether the report treats of private experiences or publicly observable occasions. (b) The audience is expected to accept these reports as true, and is free to 'check up' on them or attempt to discredit them" (*Autobiographical Acts,* p. 11).

CHAPTER THREE

1. *Invisible Man* (New York: New American Library, 1952), pp. 236–37.

2. "Richard Wright's Blues," in *Shadow and Act* (New York: New American Library, 1966), p. 92.

3. "The Psychological Reactions of Oppressed People," in *White Man, Listen!,* pp. 4–5. *White Man, Listen!* first appeared in 1957. All citations in my text refer to the 1964 edition.

4. It was at Bandung that Asian and African artists, diplomats, and political leaders first conceived of their territories and concerns as those of a "Third World." Richard Wright has rendered a fascinating account of Bandung in *The Colour Curtain* (London: Dennis Dobson, 1956).

5. I have relied on several works for broad historical details of the period 1954–76. These included Lerone Bennett, Jr., *Before the Mayflower;* John Hope Franklin, *The Negro in the Making of America* (New York: Collier, 1968); John Hope Franklin, "A Brief History," in Mabel M. Smythe, ed., *The Black American Reference Book* (Englewood Cliffs, N.J.: Prentice-Hall, 1976), pp. 1–89.

6. James Baldwin, *Notes of a Native Son* (Boston: Beacon, 1962), pp. 20–21, 29–30. *Notes* was first published in 1955.

7. *Giovanni's Room* (New York: Dell, 1974).

8. "David's dilemma is the dilemma . . . of many men of his generation; by which I do not so much mean sexual ambivalence as a crucial lack of sexual authority. A certain inability to face the world, or himself, as it is" (Fern Marya Eckman, *The Furious Passage of James Baldwin* [New York: Popular Library, 1966], p. 113).

9. Wright is here referring exclusively to Africans on the Gold Coast. His remark, however, seems to cover his general sentiments on the results of European colonialism throughout Asia and Africa.

10. *Pagan Spain* (New York: Harper, 1957), p. 240.

11. *Black Power* (New York: Harper, 1954).

12. "Blueprint for Negro Writing," *New Challenge* 1 (1937). A longer version appears in *Amistad* 2 (1971): 3–20.

13. *The Long Dream* (New York: Ace, 1958), p. 32.

14. *Savage Holiday* (New York: Award Books, 1969), p. 220.

15. "Princes and Powers," in *Nobody Knows My Name* (New York: Dell, 1968), pp. 24–54.

16. The feelings of the writers who assembled in New York are recorded in an impressive volume of essays, *The American Negro Writer and His Roots* (New York: American Society of African Culture, 1960).

17. Ibid., p. 63.

18. Ibid., p. 60.

19. Ibid., p. 16.

20. *Libretto for the Republic of Liberia* (London: Collier-Macmillan, 1970), p. 31.

CHAPTER FOUR

1. William Mahoney, "Travels in the South: A Cold Night in Alabama," in Jones and Neal, eds., *Black Fire*, pp. 144–48.

2. LeRoi Jones, *Preface to a Twenty-Volume Suicide Note* (New York: Totem Press and Corinth Books, 1961), p. 10. For a provocative critical assessment of Baraka's work, see Kimberly W. Benston's *Baraka: The Renegade and the Mask* (New Haven: Yale University Press, 1976). For a rather full biographical account, see Theodore Hudson's *From LeRoi Jones to Amiri Baraka* (Durham, N.C.: Duke University Press, 1973).

3. LeRoi Jones, *Home: Social Essays*, pp. 39–40.

4. LeRoi Jones, *Dutchman and The Slave* (New York: Morrow, 1964).

5. In *Black Magic: Poetry 1961–1967* (Indianapolis: Bobbs-Merrill, 1969), p. 55, *Black Magic* contains three groups of poems. In addition to *Target Study*, which includes poems written between 1963 and 1965, there are *Sabotage* (1961–63) and *Black Art* (1965–66).

6. LeRoi Jones, *The Dead Lecturer* (New York: Grove, 1964), p. 29.

7. LeRoi Jones, *Four Black Revolutionary Plays* (Indianapolis: Bobbs-Merrill, 1969), p. 24.

8. LeRoi Jones, *Tales* (New York: Grove, 1967), p. 87.

9. LeRoi Jones, *The System of Dante's Hell* (New York: Grove, 1966), p. 149. I am aware that Baraka says that some of the stories in *Tales* appeared earlier than 1967. Two chapters from the novel appear in Herbert Hill's controversial anthology, *Soon, One Morning* (1963). Baraka did not arrive at the "collected" vision for either work, however, until he prepared them for publication. It seems logical, therefore, to move in accord with publication dates.

10. Imamu Amiri Baraka, *Raise Race Rays Raze, Essays since 1965*, (New York: Vintage, 1972), p. 65.

11. Imamu Amiri Baraka, *Spirit Reach* (Newark: Jihad Productions, 1972), p. 11. I have chosen to disregard Baraka's infatuation with the doctrines of Ron Karenga, known as Kawaida. Kawaida stressed seven principles of a value system called the Nguzo Saba, and Baraka treats the system in *A Black Value System*. The actions and writings of the Kawaida phase, it seems to me, belong to a history of black sects and cults.

12. Imamu Amiri Baraka, "The Congress of Afrikan People: A Position Paper," *Black Scholar* 6 (1975): 9.

13. Imamu Amiri Baraka, "Needed: A Revolutionary Strategy," *Black Scholar* 7 (1975): 45. For those who wish to pursue Baraka's most recent writings, *Hard Facts* (a collection of poems written between 1973 and 1975) is available from People's War, P.O. Box 663, Newark, N.J. The same agency has also advertised release of a new collection of Baraka's essays, *Toward Ideological Clarity*. Unfortunately, *Hard Facts* is still hard to come by, and as far as I know the new essays are not yet available. *Selected Plays and Prose* and a selection of new and previously published poems were released by William Morrow late in 1979.

14. *Report from Part One* (Detroit: Broadside, 1972), pp. 84–85.

15. *Selected Poems* (New York: Harper, 1963), p. 19.

16. Ibid., p. 39.

17. *In the Mecca* (New York: Harper and Row, 1968), p. 28. The Mecca was a huge apartment building in Chicago that, at one stage in its history, was reported to contain some two thousand occupants. Ms. Brooks's poem explores what she represents as some of the lives of these occupants.

18. See my essay "The Achievement of Gwendolyn Brooks," *Singers of Daybreak* (Washington, D.C.: Howard University Press, 1974), pp. 43–51.

19. I wish to thank Professor Arnold Rampersad for sharing with me his insights on "The Wall."

20. *Riot* (Detroit: Broadside, 1969), p. 15.

21. *Beckonings* (Detroit: Broadside, 1975), p. 16.

22. *Nobody Knows My Name*, p. 11.

23. *Tell Me How Long the Train's Been Gone* (New York: Dell, 1973), p. 370.

24. *No Name in the Street* (New York: Dell, 1973), p. 9.

25. Cleaver's attack is entitled "Notes of a Native Son" and appears in *Soul on Ice* (New York: McGraw-Hill, 1968), pp. 97–111. How absurd Cleaver's attack seemed on its first appearance. And his current evangelical view of life makes it seem grotesque that anyone should have taken him seriously in the first instance. Baldwin's answer in *No Name* is a masterpiece of intellectual rebuttal.

26. *If Beale Street Could Talk* (New York: Dial, 1974).

27. The publication details of the debate between Ellison and Howe are set down in Ellison's prefatory remarks to "The World and the Jug" (*Shadow and Act*, pp. 115–47). Howe's initial essay is entitled "Black Boys and Native Sons."

28. "Opinions of a Freeman of Colour in Charleston," in Porter, ed., *Early Negro Writing*, p. 305.

29. "Petition Addressed to the Representatives of the Town of

Thompson, April 20, 1773. Signed by Peter Bestes, Sambo Freeman, Felix Holbrook."

30. *The Condition, Elevation, Emigration and Destiny of the Coloured People of the United States* (New York: Arno Press and the New York Times, 1968), p. 15. Delany is one of the most fascinating black spokesmen of the nineteenth century. For a treatment of his life and works, see Cyril E. Griffith, *The African Dream* (University Park and London: Pennsylvania State University Press, 1975).

31. *Dusk of Dawn: An Essay toward an Autobiography of a Race Concept* (New York: Schocken, 1968), pp. 199–200. For a lucid account of Du Bois's thought, see Arnold Rampersad, *The Art and Imagination of W. E. B. Du Bois* (Cambridge, Mass.: Harvard University Press, 1976).

32. "And Shine Swam On," in Jones and Neal, eds., *Black Fire*, p. 653.

33. Ibid., p. 655. Eric Wolf discusses the concept of the "cultural performance" in *Anthropology* (Englewood Cliffs, N.J.: Prentice-Hall, 1964), pp. 75–76. Using Milton Singer's *Traditional India* (particularly an essay by Norvin Hein) as reference, he says: "Where previous research into Indian religion and cosmology or sacred literature had focused almost exclusively on the study of sacred texts or artistic products, the understanding of these works could now be set in the enormously enriched context of larger 'cultural performances' in which they received expression and life . . . a performance that provides a ritual statement of the solidarity and continuity of . . . culture . . . . Such 'cultural performances,' exemplified further by weddings, temple festivals, dances, or musical performances, may be seen as constituting culturally standardized sequences of communication" (pp. 75–76).

34. One of the clearer definitions of *register* comes from: M. A. K. Halliday and Ruquaiya Hasen, *Cohesion in English*, pp. 21–26. Discussing the nature of narrative texts, the authors note the importance of what they call the "context of situation." Since every genre has its own discourse structure and is surrounded by culturally established and highly valued norms, the process of analyzing a text from any particular genre must include some attention to its contextual or situational meanings. *Field, mode,* and *tenor* are all aspects of such meaning and come together under the sign *register*. An understanding of the "texture" of any discourse structure relies, in part, on the reader's knowledge of its register. The coherence of a text depends not only on its internal cohesiveness (i.e., its coherence with respect to itself), but also on its consistency of register. In order to grasp the character of the text-forming process, in other words, one must grasp both its semantic-situational coherence and its cohesiveness. The appeal here is far more sociolinguistic than "New Critical." And I think that is precisely the point for Neal. He

is more interested in social or cultural contexts as a source of meaning and value than in an idealized arrangement of words and sentences that is assumed to have artistic value simply because it possesses internal cohesion. By appealing to more "public" discourse structures, Neal insists upon different norms in the "context of situation" of black literary texts. When he speaks of "destroying" the text, he is actually speaking of importing expectations and values from other realms of discourse to a literary domain. He does not have in mind a book burning.

35. In *The Study of Folklore* (Englewood Cliffs, N.J.: Prentice-Hall, 1965), Alan Dundes writes: "One must remember that in most of the cultures of the world, *all* the information culturally defined as important is passed on orally. In some cultures, special individuals are selected, formally or informally, to be the repositories of oral tradition. In others, individuals simply assume the responsibility on their own" (p. 217). Referring to the work of C. W. von Sydow, he continues: "Active bearers of tradition are those individuals who tell the tales and sing the songs. They may be contrasted with passive bearers of tradition who merely listen to the performance of active bearers" (p. 219). Cultural performance, the register of folk and popular discourse, and the concept of the active tradition bearer all combine in Neal's formulations, presenting an idea of the black writer far removed from the genteel apologetics seen at the outset of Vassa's narrative. What one can extrapolate from Neal's remarks, I think, are the rules, or appropriateness conditions, for black nationalist literary acts. One can certainly infer the "context of situation" for black nationalist literary discourse.

36. The discussion of the white American response to black nationalist impulses in recent years relies heavily on Alphonso Pinkney's *Red, Black, and Green: Black Nationalism in the United States* (Cambridge: Cambridge University Press, 1976).

37. Ibid., p. 230.

38. Ibid., p. 223.

CHAPTER FIVE

1. Books, collections, and articles that move toward a statement of the Black Aesthetic are: the essays on literature and language in Jones's *Home: Social Essays;* Neal's "The Black Arts Movement," in Gayle, ed., *The Black Aesthetic,* pp. 272–90; Lee's (now Haki Madhubuti's) *Dynamite Voices* (Detroit: Broadside, 1971); Jones and Neal's *Black Fire;* Addison Gayle, Jr.'s, *Black Aesthetic;* and a number of articles in *Black World* (formerly *Negro Digest*).

2. See Elmer Holenstein, *Roman Jakobson's Approach to Language,* trans. Catherine Schelbert and Tarcisius Schelbert (Bloomington: Indiana University Press, 1976), pp. 153–55.

3. *Black Fire,* pp. viii, xviii.

4. Gayle, ed., *The Black Aesthetic*, p. 272. Neal's essay first appeared in the *Drama Review* 12 (1968). It contains a provocative analysis of Baraka's dramatic works.

5. Ibid., p. xxiii.

6. The critical formulations of the authors mentioned include: Brawley's *The Negro in Literature and Art* (1918); Locke's *The New Negro* (1925); Wright's *White Man, Listen!* (1957); Ellison's *Shadow and Act* (1954); Butcher's *The Negro in American Culture* (1956). There have always been black critics who have stood outside this prospect as well. Sterling Brown and Darwin Turner come to mind.

7. Caudwell's *Illusion and Reality* (New York: International Publishers, 1973) was first published in 1937. According to Caudwell, "I, the artist, have a certain consciousness, represented by the direct and indirect effect on me of all the art I have felt, and all the emotional organisation which has produced in me a conscious subject. This consciousness is contradicted by my experience—that is, I have a *new* personal experience, something not given in the social world of poetry. Therefore I desire what is called self-expression but is really self-socialization, the casting of my private experience in such a form that it will be incorporated in the social world of art and appear as an art work. The art work represents the negation of the negation—the synthesis between the existing world of art (existing consciousness or theory) and my experience (life or practice)" (p. 224). In *Voices in the Whirlwind* (New York: Hill and Wang, 1972), Mphahlele writes: "The writing of a poem or fiction or a play is, at a level relevant to us, an act of objectifying one's subjective experience and making it publicly available. If I tell you, 'I'm angry,' I am not expressing anything like what I really feel, if I am sincere. The best way to approximate the actual thing that is going on inside me is to objectify the emotion, represent it through imagery, suggestive language sparked off by objects, characters, or actors, and so on" (p. 80).

8. *The Black Aesthetic*, p. xxi.

9. "Blackness Can: A Quest for Aesthetics," in Jones and Neal, eds., *Black Fire*, pp. 192–223. The quoted sentence is found on p. 221. This article is one of the more analytical and persuasive comments to emerge from the Black Aesthetic camp. When I say "like Ellison" in the next sentence, I am referring to Ralph Ellison's essay "Hidden Name and Complex Fate," found in *Shadow and Act*.

CHAPTER SIX

1. See *The Intricate Knot*.

2. *Notes on the State of Virginia*, p. 140.

3. Winthrop Jordan, *White over Black* (Chapel Hill: University of North Carolina Press, 1968), p. 110. "It seems almost as if the Negro had become a counter image for the European, a vivid reminder of

the dangers facing transplanted Europeans, the living embodiment of what they must never allow themselves to become."

4. Philip S. Foner, *Frederick Douglass* (New York: Citadel, 1969), p. 142.

5. Quoted from Bruce Jackson, ed., *The Negro and His Folklore in Nineteenth-Century Periodicals* (Austin: University of Texas Press, 1967), pp. 147–48. Owens's remark appeared first in *Lippincott Magazine*.

6. "Uncle Remus and the Malevolent Rabbit," *Commentary* 7 (July 1969): 31.

7. *The Literary History of the American Revolution, 1763–1783* (New York: Frederick Ungar, 1957), 1:187–88.

8. In one of the most ill informed essays ever written by a white man about black America, Robert F. Moss declares that black American creativity is not only sparse (i.e., his very brief chronology of black cultural achievements), but also wholly imitative of norms set by whites. His article appeared in the November 15, 1975, issue of *Saturday Review*. Stephen Henderson offers a fine critique of Moss in "The Question of Form and Judgment in Contemporary Black American Poetry," which appears in *A Dark and Sudden Beauty: Two Essays in Black American Poetry*, ed. Houston A. Baker, Jr., Afro-American Studies Program, University of Pennsylvania (Philadelphia, 1977), pp. 20–21. Henderson's essay is valuable for an understanding of the entire question of critical evaluation vis-à-vis black literature.

9. *A Literary History of America* (New York: Scribner, 1900), p. 482.

10. Quoted from Helen M. Chesnutt, *Charles Waddell Chesnutt: Pioneer of the Color Line* (Chapel Hill: University of North Carolina Press, 1952), p. 177. Howells's comment originally appeared in "A Psychological Counter-Current in Recent Fiction," *North American Review*, December 1901.

11. Howells set this range in his introduction to Dunbar's *Lyrics of Lowly Life*. See *The Complete Poems of Paul Laurence Dunbar* (New York: Dodd-Mead, 1913), p. ix.

12. *The Negro Character in American Literature* (Lawrence, Kan., 1926), p. 23. Nelson is quoted here from Seymour L. Gross and John Edward Hardy, eds., *Images of the Negro in American Literature* (Chicago: University of Chicago Press, 1966), p. 5.

CHAPTER SEVEN

1. Books, articles, and sections of texts dealing with the language of black Americans include: Juanita Williamson, "Selected Features of Speech: Black and White," *CLA Journal*, June 1970; Kirkland Jones's "The Language of the Black 'In-Crowd': Some Observations on Intra-Group Communications," *CLA Journal*, September 1971;

J. L. Dillard, *Black English* (New York: Random House, 1972); Orlando Taylor, "Historical Development of Black English and Implications for American Education," in Ronald Williams and Richard Ham, eds., *Speech and Language of the Urban and Rural Poor,* Summer Institute on Speech and Language of the Urban and Rural Poor, Ohio University, Athens, Ohio, July 14–16, 1969; Philip S. Dale, *Language Development* (Hinsdale, Ill.: Dryden Press, 1972), pp. 244–54; Victoria Fromkin and Robert Rodman, *An Introduction to Language* (New York: Holt, Rinehart, and Winston, 1974), pp. 258–69; William Labov, *Language in the Inner City: Studies in the Black English Vernacular* (Philadelphia: University of Pennsylvania Press, 1972). One of the pioneering studies in this area was Lorenzo Turner's *Africanisms in the Gullah Dialect* (New York: Arno, 1969). One of the most recent works is Geneva Smitherman, *Talkin and Testifyin: The Language of Black America* (Boston: Houghton Mifflin, 1977). On the general topic of pidgin and creole languages, one can consult Albert Valdman, ed., *Pidgin and Creole Linguistics* (Bloomington: Indiana University Press, 1977).

2. The linguist Edward Sapir and his student Benjamin Lee Whorf are often credited with a philosophy (or an analytical point of view) that stresses linguistic determinism. Both were advocates of the notion that "human beings do not live in the objective world alone, nor alone in the world of social activity as ordinarily understood, but are very much at the mercy of the particular language which has become the medium of expression for their society. It is quite an illusion to imagine that one adjusts to reality essentially without the use of language and that language is merely an incidental means of solving specific problems of communication or reflection. The fact of the matter is that the 'real world' is to a large extent unconsciously built up on the language habits of the group. No two languages are ever sufficiently similar to be considered as representing the same social reality" (Sapir, "The Status of Linguistics as a Science," in *Culture, Language and Personality: Selected Essays,* ed. David G. Mandelbaum [Berkeley: University of California Press, 1949], p. 69). By this notion, intercultural communication would be an enormously difficult task because the underlying "cryptotypes" (basic grammatical categories) of any one culture's language would be totally at odds with those of other cultures. Writing on the Hopi Indians, Whorf emphasizes the interpenetration of language and reality; the world view of the Hopi is coded into their language and differs significantly from that of Anglo-American speakers of English (see John B.Carroll., ed., *Language, Thought and Reality,* a collection of Whorf's essays, MIT Press, 1956). There is much that is suggestive in the "Sapir-Whorf hypothesis," and my point is not to discount the notion. I simply wish to indicate that the African's or the Afro-American's acquisition of English did not subject him or her

to the "world view" of the European in the automatic, deterministic way that the Sapir-Whorf hypothesis might suggest. Only on the assumption that Africans were without "language" when they encountered the West would such a position be remotely tenable. Moreover, the more detailed work on "speech communities" undertaken by linguists like Dell Hymes and William Labov in recent years suggests that there is far more variation—even in a single community—than Sapir and Whorf seemed ready to allow. While the earlier investigators emphasized "determinism," today's scholars of "pragmatics" seem more interested in free variation. One act of "freedom," theorize Ludwig Wittgenstein and certain symbolic anthropologists, is negation. The native speaker can move against the grain of positive, descriptive linguistic categories by inverting or negating them. The range of freedom thus includes irony, paradox, and other verbal strategies that are not exclusively communicative or informational speech acts. Ultimately, one is concerned with the "psychological reality" underlying language use, and as yet there is no definitive model. It seems reasonable to assume, however, that human symbolic behavior is at least an admixture of predetermined and innovative forms and processes. Under this view, adult African speakers could certainly be conceived of as playing manifold variations on the "themes" laid down by European vocabulary items.

3. *Philosophical Investigations,* trans. G. E. M. Anscome (New York: Macmillan, 1953), p. 118e. My notion of Wittgenstein's point of view derives from my interpretation of sections 243–415. For an elaboration of Wittgenstein's philosophy, see Jeffrey T. Price, *Language and Being in Wittgenstein's "Philosophical Investigations"* (The Hague: Mouton, 1973).

4. "Refugee in America," in *Selected Poems of Langston Hughes* (New York: Knopf, 1969), p. 290.

5. *Race and Nationality in American Life* (Boston: Little, Brown, 1947), pp. 71–92.

6. *The Slave Community* (New York: Oxford University Press, 1973), p. 45.

7. See my *Long Black Song,* pp. 122–41.

8. "Fever and Feeling: Notes on the Imagery of *Native Son,*" *Negro Digest* 18 (1968): 16–24.

9. "Generative Semantics and Literary Discourse," *Journal of Literary Semantics* 2 (1973): 6.

10. The structural linguists—notably Roman Jakobson—considered the phoneme the minimal unit of language that native speakers recognize as meaningful. For example, "bat" and "pat" would be seen by speakers of English as lexical items with different meanings on the basis of the differing phonemes /b/ and /p/. Analyzing such instances, the structuralists concluded that a

phoneme could be either "plus consonantal" or "minus consonantal," "plus nasal" or "minus nasal," "plus voiced" or "minus voiced," and so on. The "meaning" of a phoneme (and consequently of the morphemes, lexemes, and sentences into which it combined) was therefore a function of relationships of "binary opposition." Basing his work on what he termed the "phonological revolution" brought about by structural linguistics, the anthropologist Claude Lévi-Strauss sought to analyze myths in terms of their minimal meaningful units and the relationships into which they entered (see Lévi-Strauss, *Structural Anthropology* [New York: Basic, 1976]). In his suggestive essay on the Oedipal myth, Lévi-Strauss isolated what he saw as fundamental variables and deftly illustrated how the relationships among these variables revealed underlying generative principles and provided an extended interpretation of the myth's meaning (see Culler, *Structuralist Poetics,* pp. 40–54). When I use the term *binary relationship,* I am invoking the history just discussed. But since the structural linguists, anthropologists, and folklorists who have followed Lévi-Strauss's lead have not only posited "structural relationships" but also argued for the autonomous character of language, culture, and myth as "structured systems," I must qualify my usage. Rather than arguing for the self-contained character of a system embodying its own generative and transformational rules, I am suggesting that the discovery of a fundamental structural relationship comprises a beginning rather than an end. Only when such "discoveries" are integrated into a full analytical context are they suggestive for one's understanding of actual human beings and their cultures. The designation of a structural relationship in chapter eleven, in other words, is in the service of a fuller analysis of black American literature and culture. It is an interpretive strategy in the larger enterprise that I call the anthropology of art.

11. For an elaboration of this point of view, as well as its converse, see the essays of Howard Mumford Jones and Peter Drucker in Melvin Kranzberg and William H. Davenport, eds., *Technology and Culture* (New York: New American Library, 1972).

12. J. Huizinga's *Homo Ludens* (London: Routledge and Kegan Paul, 1949) is still one of the more provacative works on culture as play. The analysis of culture and play is currently the focus of the Society for the Anthropological Study of Play. There are informative essays on the subject in Edward Norbeck, ed., *The Anthropological Study of Human Play, Rice University Studies* 60 (1974).

13. The anthropologist Victor Turner explores the concept of "liminality" in *International Encyclopedia of the Social Sciences,* s.v. "Myth and Symbol." Basing his formulations on Arnold van Gennep's *The Rites of Passage* (1909), Turner provides a suggestive view of the margin (or limen) that exists between the pre- and postritual

stages of rites of passage: "The individual or group undergoing *rites de passage* is, during the liminal period, neither here nor there but in limbo. The individual initiand is no longer the incumbent of a culturally defined social position or status but has not yet become the incumbent of another." Such periods are not without structure, Turner argues, but rather are times in which structure is simplified and generalized. The essential relationship is the dyad comprising the instructor and the instructee. It is a time for learning through myth and symbol as the initiand is ritualistically presented with the lore of the culture. Social segmentations of rank and status are suspended in the liminal period, and "the loss of status may be emblematized by ritual nudity, or the group's social homogeneity may be emphasized by the wearing of some uniform ritual decoration or dress. The passive attitude of male initiands may be symbolized by the wearing of female apparel. The absence of status distinctions may be shown further by the use of postures expressive of humility or by decorating the body with earth or ashes." With the dropping away of rigorous and constraining social norms, the occupant of the liminal zone is capable of seeing the fundamental principles of society. He becomes aware of "all positions and arrangements" and has a "total perspective." Moreover, the presentation of myths in the liminal phase allows for an "acting out" of socially or morally reprehensible behaviors such as those of, say, the trickster in Winnebago myths: "In myth is a limitless freedom, a symbolic freedom of action which is denied to the norm-bound incumbent of a status in a social structure." The protagonist of Ellison's *Invisible Man* enters the liminal phase of his rite of passage (a naming ceremony) with the opening lines of chapter eleven. When he identifies himself with the trickster rabbit, he has clearly defined himself as a liminal personality whose "untrammeled and unchanneled" energies are potentially, in Turner's phrase, "the source of new substances and beings." In *Culture and Communication* (Cambridge: Cambridge University Press, 1976), Edmund Leach also provides an informative and suggestive account of "rites of transition" (pp. 77–79). See also Turner's contribution to Norbeck, ed., *The Anthropological Study of Human Play*, pp. 53–92, and his essay in Babcock, ed., *The Reversible World*, pp. 276–96.

14. See Babcock, Introduction, *The Reversible World*, for a further discussion of symbolic inversion and rites of reversal (pp. 13–36).

15. I have argued for the "treadmill" or recurrent effect of the novel's motifs in "A Forgotten Prototype: *The Autobiography of an Ex-Coloured Man* and *Invisible Man*," *Singers of Daybreak: Studies in Black American Literature* (Washington, D.C.: Howard University Press, 1974), pp. 17–31.

16. *History Is Your Own Hearbeat* (Urbana: University of Illinois Press, 1971).

CONCLUSION

1. St. Clair Drake, *The Redemption of Africa and Black Religion* (Chicago: Third World Press, 1975), pp. 12–13. Drake's complete statement on this legacy appears as an epigraph for the present volume.

2. Chinua Achebe, "Language and the Destiny of Man," in *Morning Yet on Creation Day: Essays* (Garden City, N.Y.: Anchor, 1976), p. 40.

Index